RIDICULOUS
FAVOR

RIDICULOUS FAVOR

Discover the Secrets to Attracting
UNBELIEVABLE GIFTS *from* GOD

JOHN ECKHARDT

BEST-SELLING AUTHOR OF *PRAYERS THAT ROUT DEMONS*

Ridiculous Favor by John Eckhardt
Published by John Eckhardt Ministries
PO Box 373
Olympia Fields, IL 60461
www.johneckhardt.global

Visit the author's website at www.johneckhardt.global.

International Standard Book Number: 978-1-947950-00-9
E-book ISBN: 978-1-947950-01-6

Cover design by Bill Johnson
Original art illustration by April Clark, "Gems of Favor," copyright © 2017

Created live during a July 30, 2017 praise and worship service at Crusaders Church in Chicago, IL, "Gems of Favor" is a visual depiction of a glorious vision given to the artist. In the vision, the intangible spiritual gift of favor took on the form of tangible gems that were washed in the spiritual River of Royalty. Before laying on color for the background, the Holy Spirit led the artist to wash the canvas with water to capture the River of Favor the congregation was to swim in while worshiping during the special service called Mega-Favor Sunday.

The color purple symbolizes royalty, kingship, wealth, prosperity, and luxury. When believers are favored, they have these things because King Jesus reigns.

The purple in this image was created by mixing red, which symbolizes the blood of Jesus that was shed, and blue, which symbolizes the Spirit of God and the heavenly dwelling place. Believers sit in heavenly places with Christ Jesus and are washed in favor.

"Gemstone deposits that are carried by rivers are called placers or alluvial deposits. Rivers can transport gem-bearing rock many hundreds of miles. When the force of the current diminishes, the denser gems—such as diamond, zircon, garnet, sapphire, chrysoberyl, topaz, peridot, and tourmaline—are deposited before the lighter quartz sand." (GemSelect.com)

Instead of finding gems on a dry river bed, believers will find gems in the deep rivers of the favor of God.

17 18 19 20 21 — 987654321
Printed in the United States of America

CONTENTS

RIDICULOUS FAVOR

You have granted me life and favor, and Your care has preserved my spirit.

—JOB 10:12, NKJV

F AVOR IS A major theme in the Bible. When we accept Christ, we come into covenant with the favor of God and favor then becomes a major theme in our lives. The word *favour* is found seventy times in seventy verses in the King James Version of the Bible. The word *favor* is found 293 times throughout the scriptures in the Amplified Bible. Between the two versions, *favor* is mention a total of 363 times. This number is significant and shows the importance of being in position to receive the favor of God in our lives.

Favor is defined as "approval, support, or liking for someone or something;" "an act of kindness beyond what is due or usual," to "feel or show approval or preference for; "(often used in polite request) give someone (something that they want)."[1] It means "to give special regard to; to treat with goodwill; to show exceptional kindness to someone. Sometimes, it means to show extra kindness in comparison to the treatment of others; that is, preferential treatment."[2] Favor is also "friendly regard shown toward another especially by a superior; gracious kindness; an act of such kindness; aid, assistance."[3] To a

Christian, favor with God is what He bestows upon you or gives you.

> *Get ready for an avalanche of favor.*[4]
> *—John Coleman*

When someone uses their power, influence, position, wealth, authority, and words to help and bless you, that is favor—and it doesn't depend on anything you've done. Favor is unmerited, meaning you don't deserve it but it is given to you anyway. God is a God of favor; He loves to bless His people simply because He is a good Father. In Matthew 7:11, the Bible tells us that God gives good gifts to those who ask. Favor is one of the best gifts you can receive from God. It is a demonstration that He is using His power and authority on your behalf and is manifesting His love toward you.

A TSUNAMI OF FAVOR

I believe that now is a set time for favor. A flood, a tsunami of ridiculous favor is about to hit your life.

> The Lord said to me, "I am releasing ridiculous favor and this favor I am pouring out is going to be so outrageous. My people will be laughing their way into their promises. It will spark hilarious outbreaks of My joy as I move in an unthinkable, astonishing expression of

My favor that will catapult My people in their divine destiny."[5]

—Anita Alexander

Ridiculous favor is [an] amazing, tremendous, bountiful blessing granted to God's children. We should expect a real time of favor: even to the point of being ridiculous in its scope, miraculousness and undeservedness.[6]

—Dea Warford

Get ready for the ridiculous. Get ready for ridiculous favor. *Ridiculous* is defined as "arousing or deserving ridicule, extremely silly or unreasonable, absurd, preposterous."[7] *Ridiculous* also means that which is laughable.[8]

There are many things in Scripture that would seem ridiculous to the natural man. A donkey converses with a prophet. A fish swallows a prophet and spits him out after three days. The red sea opens by the breath of God. A man is raised from the dead after being dead four days. A prophet prays and fire falls from heaven. A deliverer kills one thousand men with the jawbone of an donkey. These stories may sound ridiculous, but those who believe know that God does what seems ridiculous to man.

Miracles seem ridiculous to those who do not believe. God can and will do unbelievable things in your life. This includes giving you ridiculous favor.

I first heard the term *ridiculous favor* while doing a thirty-day teaching about favor. As I researched and studied the subject, I came across the term *ridiculous favor* several times. It was mentioned by several people and was a prophetic word to believers. When I heard the term, I immediately grabbed hold of it and began to say it. The more I pondered the term, the more it opened to me.

Although I have known about the favor of God for many years, during this thirty days of teaching, I began to see things I had not seen before. God began to give me more revelation of His favor.

There were other terms that stood out as I ministered on favor, but the term *ridiculous favor* stood out. I believe that a prophetic word can shift you into a new place of blessing and breakthrough. One word from God can turn your life around. And ridiculous favor is a turn-around word for this season.

As more and more people took to the teaching on favor, the more I felt led to write a book to capture the anointing and revelation God released to me and those who participated in the teaching. In this book, much like I did during the teaching sessions, I will discuss the benefits of God's favor and how you can increase in it. Yes, you can increase in favor:

> There are levels of favor with God. You can choose to be at a basic level of favor with Him, or you can choose to be at a high level of favor with Him.[9]
>
> —JAMIE ROHRBAUGH

You do not have to stay on the same level of favor. In Luke 2:52, it says that "Jesus increased in wisdom and stature, and in favour with God and man." As Jesus increased in favor with God and man, you can also increase in favor with God and man. No matter what level of favor you are walking in, you can go higher and increase. Through this revelation of favor, I will show you how to receive, increase in, and walk in the favor of God for a lifetime.

I believe this book will open the door for you to experience not just regular favor but ridiculous favor. This level of favor will cause you to receive what is impossible and unbelievable in the natural. What God wants to do in your life may seem absurd and unreasonable, but if you read the Bible, you will discover that this is nothing new. There are many examples in Scripture of people who were favored by God. I will examine in detail these people to inspire you to believe God for increase in favor.

I want you to know, have faith for, and experience a flood of ridiculous favor in your life. The benefits of God's favor in your life are unlimited.

- Favor can open doors.
- Favor can cause breakthrough.
- Favor can remove years of struggle in a day.
- Favor can accelerate your destiny.
- Favor can give you new opportunities.

- Favor can cause men to give you what you need.
- Favor is a shortcut to success.
- Favor can put you on new platforms.
- Favor can bring you promotion.
- Favor can make your way easier.
- Favor can give you numerous victories.
- Favor can bring the right people into your life.

Our God is the God of favor. He doesn't want to just give you a little favor; He wants to lavish His favor upon your life. I want you to get this mentality so that you can be open to receive this kind of favor no matter who you are as a believer! Let's take a closer look at how God makes this abundant gift available to all.

Part I

PREPARATION FOR A
NEW LEVEL OF FAVOR

Chapter 1

BUILDING FAITH FOR
THE RIDICULOUS

*Sometimes a step of faith and obedience is
needed before God's favor is released![1]*

—DAVID CERULLO

OD FAVORS FAITH. God favors the faithful.
Faith and faithfulness attracts the favor of
God. Without faith, it is impossible to please
God (Heb. 11:6). Faith brings God's reward upon your
life. Favor is a reward for believing God. Nothing moves
without faith. It is the currency of heaven. To receive
from God, you must have faith in God and believe Him
for favor. Confess favor. Increase your faith for favor. Do
not doubt or be double-minded concerning favor. The
Old Testament story of Abraham and Sarah teaches us
the importance of believing God for ridiculous favor.

In Genesis 17, God appeared to Abraham (then named
Abram) and told him that He would multiply him exceedingly and make him exceedingly fruitful. Along the covenant blessings we all now have access to through Christ,
God also promised Abraham that he would have a son in
his old age. There was only one problem. Abraham was

one hundred years old, and his wife, Sarah (then Sarai), was ninety. Sarah's womb was dead.

Abraham and Sarah both laughed when they heard this promised. They laughed because they thought that the promise was ridiculous.

> Then Abraham fell upon his face, and laughed, and said in his heart, Shall a child be born unto him that is an hundred years old? and shall Sarah, that is ninety years old, bear?
>
> —GENESIS 17:17

> Now Abraham and Sarah were old and well stricken in age; and it ceased to be with Sarah after the manner of women.
>
> Therefore Sarah laughed within herself, saying, After I am waxed old shall I have pleasure, my lord being old also?
>
> And the LORD said unto Abraham, Wherefore did Sarah laugh, saying, Shall I of a surety bear a child, which am old?
>
> —GENESIS 18:11–13

> Is any thing too hard for the LORD? At the time appointed I will return unto thee, according to the time of life, and Sarah shall have a son.
>
> Then Sarah denied, saying, I laughed not; for she was afraid. And he said, Nay; but thou didst laugh.
>
> —GENESIS 18:14–15

Sarah denied that she laughed, but she did. She thought that what she heard was laughable. She thought that what she heard was ridiculous. It was, but still the word of the Lord came to pass. Isaac was born from the union of Abraham and Sarah. What seemed ridiculous came to pass. The Bible says that "through faith also Sara herself received strength to conceive seed, and was delivered of a child when she was past age, because she judged him faithful who had promised. Therefore sprang there even of one, and him as good as dead, so many as the stars of the sky in multitude, and as the sand which is by the sea shore innumerable" (Heb. 11:11–12).

> *The favor of God will turn it in your favor.[2]*
> —E. A. Deckard

Sarah received strength for the ridiculous. Her barren womb conceived. She delivered a child when she was past child-bearing age. Isaac was the child of promise. What she had laughed about actually happened.

Romans 4:19–20 records that Abraham believed God for the ridiculous to happen, and it happened:

And being not weak in faith, he considered not his own body now dead, when he was about an hundred years old, neither yet the deadness of Sarah's womb: He staggered not at the promise of God through unbelief; but was strong in faith, giving glory to God.

Notice that the scripture says Abraham was not weak in faith. He was strong in faith and gave glory to God. He did not stagger at the promise of God through unbelief. And by his strong faith, Abraham became the father of many nations.

Has God ever shown you something that seemed ridiculous? Has he ever spoke ridiculous things into your life? A ridiculous dream or prophetic word? Faith can bring the ridiculous things into manifestation. Faith causes the impossible to become possible.

When God gives you a promise, do not stagger through unbelief. It may sound ridiculous. You may even laugh when you hear it. But God is the God who does ridiculous things. Faith in His promise will cause that which seems ridiculous to come to pass.

Favor will cause ridiculous things to happen for you. Favor will open ridiculous doors. Favor will give you ridiculous opportunities. Favor will bring you ridiculous breakthroughs. Favor will give you ridiculous promotions and advance. Favor will give you ridiculous connections. Receive faith for the ridiculous as you continue to more stories of ridiculous favor.

RIDICULOUS FAVOR RAISES THE DEAD TO LIFE

Do you have areas in your life that are dead or dormant? Begin to stir up new faith for God to bring them back to life. If He did it before, know that it is available to you right now today. See in Mark chapter 5, where Jesus came into the house of a child who had died. When He got in the room, He said, "She is not dead, but asleep."

> And when he was come in, he saith unto them, Why make ye this ado, and weep? the damsel is not dead, but sleepeth.
>
> And they laughed him to scorn. But when he had put them all out, he taketh the father and the mother of the damsel, and them that were with him, and entereth in where the damsel was lying.
>
> And he took the damsel by the hand, and said unto her, Talitha cumi; which is, being interpreted, Damsel, I say unto thee, arise.
>
> —MARK 5:39–41

The people laughed him to scorn. In other words, "What You just said is ridiculous. She is obviously dead." Jesus then put them out and said to the young lady, "Arise." The young lady arose.

> And straightway the damsel arose, and walked; for she was of the age of twelve years. And they were astonished with a great astonishment.
>
> —MARK 5:42

The people were astonished. *Astonish* means "to strike with sudden and usually great wonder or surprise."[3] They were all surprised. They went from laughter and scorn to surprise.

Is this a word for you? Are there dreams and visions

that you thought were dead? Is God telling you that they are not dead, only asleep and waiting for the word of the Lord to come and say, "Arise"? I believe that God is doing astonishing things in the lives of His people. I believe that He is speaking to dead and dormant areas and saying, "Arise!" God desires to surprise His people with astonishing miracles. This is what ridiculous favor will do for your life.

Lazarus

Another astonishing miracle Jesus performed was in raising Lazarus from the dead. Lazarus had been dead four days.

> Jesus said, Take ye away the stone. Martha, the sister of him that was dead, saith unto him, Lord, by this time he stinketh: for he hath been dead four days.
>
> —JOHN 11:39

Jesus told them to roll the stone away. Martha responded by saying, "By this time he stinks." In other words, "This is a ridiculous command. He has been dead for too long."

No one had ever seen anyone raised from the dead after four days, but Lazarus did come forth. This was one of the greatest miracles ever seen. Lazarus had died and was already buried.

And when they heard of the resurrection of the dead, some mocked: and others said, We will hear thee again of this matter.

—Acts 17:32

Many thought that the resurrection from the dead was ridiculous. They mocked when they heard the news of the resurrection. Multitudes believed the message. Multitudes believe it today. What is ridiculous to some is not ridiculous to the believer. God can and will do ridiculous miracles on the behalf of His people.

Unbelievable, Strange, and Remarkable Works of Favor

God spoke a word to Israel through the prophet Habakkuk. God would do a work in their day that was unbelievable, that God would work a work among the heathen.

Behold ye among the heathen, and regard, and wonder marvelously: for I will work a work in your days which ye will not believe, though it be told you.

—Habakkuk 1:5

Strange and remarkable

God often does things that are remarkable and ridiculous. God often does a strange work and a strange act.

For the LORD shall rise up as in mount Perazim, he shall be wroth as in the valley of Gibeon, that he may

> do his work, his strange work; and bring to pass his act,
> his strange act.
>
> —ISAIAH 28:21

Conversation with a donkey

God spoke to Balaam through a donkey. This is indeed ridiculous. Donkeys don't talk. Balaam even had a conversation with the donkey.

> And the LORD opened the mouth of the ass, and she
> said unto Balaam, What have I done unto thee, that
> thou hast smitten me these three times?
>
> —NUMBERS 22:28

Some would say this is ridiculous to carry on a conversation with a donkey, but God used the donkey to speak in a man's voice.

> But was rebuked for his iniquity: the dumb ass speaking
> with man's voice forbad the madness of the prophet.
>
> —2 PETER 2:16

Ridiculous conception

One of the most ridiculous manifestations of God's ability and favor is seen in the life of Mary. What is more ridiculous than God telling a young woman she would have a child without knowing a man?

> Then said Mary unto the angel, How shall this be, seeing
> I know not a man?

And the angel answered and said unto her, The Holy Ghost shall come upon thee, and the power of the Highest shall overshadow thee: therefore also that holy thing which shall be born of thee shall be called the Son of God....For with God nothing shall be impossible.

And Mary said, Behold the handmaid of the Lord; be it unto me according to thy word. And the angel departed from her.

—LUKE 1:34–35, 37–38

There are many miracles in the Bible that we can consider to be ridiculous. God does things for His people that seem ridiculous to the natural mind.

My desire is that you walk in a level of favor that will boggle your natural mind. I want to see you enter the realm of unbelievable, remarkable, and ridiculous favor. Let God release ridiculous favor in your life. Ridiculous favor is laughable favor. Ridiculous favor is abundant favor. Ridiculous favor is favor beyond what you can ask or think.

Now unto him that is able to do exceeding abundantly above all that we ask or think, according to the power that worketh in us,

—EPHESIANS 3:20

Chapter 2

THE KING'S FAVOR

A day of favor will change your life forever.[1]

—DAVE MARTIN

I T MAY SEEM obvious why you would want an abundance of favor to come upon your life, but favor is not only about having our fleshly desires fulfilled. Favor is about our having the grace and blessing of God on our lives so strongly that we are able to do greater works than Jesus did and to be in the right positions to expand the kingdom, bring glory to God, and to bring others into position to also receive favor from God. One aspect of favor is when someone uses their power, position, influence, wealth, gifts, or words to bless you and help you advance toward your dreams and goals. But there is another level of favor—the Kings' favor—that we need in this hour.

> *God's favor brings forth restoration of everything that the enemy has stolen from you.*[2]
> —Michelle McClain-Walters

Kings have the greatest amount of power and authority, and there are examples in Scripture of those who received the king's favor. Jesus is the King of kings. Jesus is the greatest King. We should all want and desire the King's favor. The level of favor that He gives us to accomplish His will in the earth and bring glory to His name is above and beyond anything that we could ask or imagine. This is the King's favor. The King's favor is ridiculous favor. This is the favor that we should seek after.

> Many seek the ruler's favour; but every man's judgment cometh from the LORD.
>
> —PROVERBS 29:26

Throughout history, many have wanted and desires their king's favor. The king's favor can be the difference between life or death. The king's favor can mean the difference between promotion or demotion. The king's favor can be the difference between success and failure. In the lives of Queen Esther and the prophet Nehemiah, the king's favor was what stood between the life and death of God's chosen people.

THE KING'S FAVOR APPOINTS A QUEEN

In the Book of Esther, it's recorded how Esther needed the king's favor to deliver her people from the evil plan of Haman. Esther risked her life going into the presence of the king uninvited. The difference between us and Esther is that we are invited to come boldly to the throne of grace.

> And the king loved Esther above all the women, and she obtained grace and favour in his sight more than all the

virgins; so that he set the royal crown upon her head, and made her queen instead of Vashti.

—ESTHER 2:17

And it was so, when the king saw Esther the queen standing in the court, that she obtained favour in his sight: and the king held out to Esther the golden sceptre that was in his hand. So Esther drew near, and touched the top of the sceptre.

—ESTHER 5:2

Esther had the favor of the King of kings before she went into the palace. The Persian king's favor was secondary. It was God's favor that was a key in Esther becoming queen. Esther was an orphan being raised by her uncle Mordecai. She was one of the many beautiful women who were vying to become the next queen. What made Esther stand out? What distinguished her from the other women? It was the King's favor. Favor will make you stand out from the crowd. Favor will distinguish you.

Now when the turn of Esther, the daughter of Abihail the uncle of Mordecai, who had taken her for his daughter, was come to go in unto the king, she required nothing but what Hegai the king's chamberlain, the keeper of the women, appointed. And Esther obtained favour in the sight of all them that looked upon her.

—ESTHER 2:15

The king extended the golden scepter to Esther when she came into his presence. The king granted her request. She received the favor of the king.

> All the king's servants, and the people of the king's provinces, do know, that whosoever, whether man or women, shall come unto the king into the inner court, who is not called, there is one law of his to put him to death, except such to whom the king shall hold out the golden sceptre, that he may live: but I have not been called to come in unto the king these thirty days.
>
> —ESTHER 4:11

> And it was so, when the king saw Esther the queen standing in the court, that she obtained favour in his sight: and the king held out to Esther the golden sceptre that was in his hand. So Esther drew near, and touched the top of the sceptre.
>
> —ESTHER 5:2

> Then the king held out the golden sceptre toward Esther. So Esther arose, and stood before the king.
>
> —ESTHER 8:4

Esther asked the king for favor and received it. In a later chapter I am going to discuss the importance of asking for favor.

> Then Esther the queen answered and said, If I have found favour in thy sight, O king, and if it please the

king, let my life be given me at my petition, and my people at my request.

—ESTHER 7:3

We can come boldly to the throne of grace. Grace is favor. The king's throne is a throne of favor. The scepter is extended toward you as a believer. You can walk in and receive the king's favor.

THE KING'S FAVOR REBUILDS WALLS

Nehemiah received favor from the king and returned to Jerusalem to rebuild the walls of the city. The king granted Nehemiah's request. But again notice that Nehemiah first sought God in prayer to receive His favor. (See Nehemiah 1:4–11.) He then knew that if he had the King's favor, he would also be granted the earthly king's favor.

And I said unto the king, If it please the king, and if thy servant have found favour in thy sight, that thou wouldest send me unto Judah, unto the city of my fathers' sepulchres, that I may build it.

—NEHEMIAH 2:5

Favor is therefore a part of restoration. Favor will bring restoration to your life. Favor can cause the walls of your life to be rebuilt.

Then I told them how the hand of my God had been favorable to me and also about the words that the king had spoken to me. And they said, "Let us rise up and build." So they thoroughly supported the good work.

—Nehemiah 2:18, amp

Nehemiah reminded the builders of the king's favor. The people rose up and built. We can build with the favor of God.

The King's Favor Sets the Table

David was a king that showed favor. He looked for a descendant of Jonathan, his covenant brother, to show favor to. David's men found Mephibosheth. Mephibosheth was lame in his feet.

And David said, Is there yet any that is left of the house of Saul, that I may shew him kindness for Jonathan's sake?

—2 Samuel 9:1

And the king said, Is there not yet any of the house of Saul, that I may shew the kindness of God unto him? And Ziba said unto the king, Jonathan hath yet a son, which is lame on his feet.

—2 Samuel 9:3

David restored the land of Saul to Mephibosheth and brought him to his table to eat. This is favor. This is the favor of a king.

And David said unto him, Fear not: for I will surely shew thee kindness for Jonathan thy father's sake, and

will restore thee all the land of Saul thy father; and thou
shalt eat bread at my table continually.

—2 SAMUEL 9:7

THE KING'S FAVOR BRINGS PROMOTION

God gave Joseph favor and wisdom in the sight of
Pharaoh, king of Egypt: "...and He rescued him from
all his suffering, and gave him favor and wisdom in the
sight of Pharaoh, king of Egypt, and he made Joseph governor over Egypt and over his entire household" (Acts
7:10, AMP).

Favor promoted Joseph to be governor over Egypt.
This passage also reveals the connection between wisdom
and favor, which I will discuss in the next chapter. The
king's favor can bring promotion. Genesis 39:21 says,

> But the LORD was with Joseph, and shewed him mercy,
> and gave him favour in the sight of the keeper of the
> prison.

Daniel received favor from the king and was promoted.
He was a stranger in a foreign land, yet favor promoted
him.

> Now God had brought Daniel into favour and tender
> love with the prince of the eunuchs.

—DANIEL 1:9

> Then this Daniel was preferred above the presidents and princes, because an excellent spirit was in him; and the king thought to set him over the whole realm.
>
> —Daniel 6:3

Daniel had an excellent spirit. I believe excellence can attract favor. Excellence is the state of being very good or superior. Excellence will make you stand out. Daniel stood out. His wisdom and his gift made him stand out.

> A man's gift maketh room for him, and bringeth him before great men.
>
> —Proverbs 18:16

Your gift will make room for you and make you stand out. You must guard, develop, cultivate, and stir up your gift. Your gifts are given to you by grace.

Forsake All and Receive the King's Favor

Ruth is another great example of receiving favor. She was a Moabite widow in a strange land. God gave her favor with Boaz. God delights in giving favor to the underdog. Ruth forsook all to follow Naomi and the God of Israel. Those who forsake all to follow Christ will experience ridiculous favor.

> Then she said, Let me find favour in thy sight, my lord; for that thou hast comforted me, and for that thou hast

spoken friendly unto thine handmaid, though I be not like unto one of thine handmaidens.

—RUTH 2:13

And let fall also some of the handfuls of purpose for her, and leave them, that she may glean them, and rebuke her not.

—RUTH 2:16

IN THE KING'S FAVOR IS LIFE

In the light of the king's countenance is life; and his favour is as a cloud of the latter rain.

—PROVERBS 16:15

The King's favor is like a cloud of the latter rain. The latter rain would come before the harvest. Rain represents abundance, fruitfulness and prosperity. Lack of clouds and rain symbolize dryness, and barrenness. The King's countenance is life. The King's countenance is the glory of God in the face of Jesus. The King causes His face to shine upon us. This is the favor of the King.

The king's wrath is as the roaring of a lion; but his favour is as dew upon the grass.

—PROVERBS 19:12

The King's favor is like the dew upon the grass. Grass needs moisture to grow. The dew is what falls upon the grass in the morning. The dew brings moisture into our lives. Favor will cause you to grow and speak up. We should wake up every morning with the dew of heaven. We should arise every day with the favor of God.

Psalm 30:5 compares the length of time that God is angry to how long His favor lasts in our lives: "For his anger endureth but a moment; in his favour is life: weeping may endure for a night, but joy cometh in the morning." His anger is for a moment, but His favor is for a lifetime. I believe you can walk in God's favor all of your life.

Simply put, grace is favor.[3]
—Gloria Copeland

The Hebrew word for "life" in Psalm 30:5 is *chay*, which is a derivative of *chayah*, meaning "to have life," "to continue in life, remain alive," "sustain life," "to live (prosperously)," "to quicken, revive, refresh," "to preserve alive," "to cause to grow," "to restore to life," and "to restore to health."[4] In other words, favor is a key to living prosperously and being alive and refreshed. Favor will keep you alive. Favor is for living. You can experience God's favor in every season of your life. You can have God's favor at a young age. This favor can continue throughout your life. Other Bible versions translate Psalm 30:5 this way:

> For his anger lasts only a brief moment, and his good favor restores one's life. One may experience sorrow during the night, but joy arrives in the morning.
>
> —NET

19

For his wrath is only momentary; yet his favor is for a lifetime. Weeping may lodge for the night, but shouts of joy will come in the morning.

—ISV

Job 10:12 is another verse that connect life to favor: "Thou hast granted me life and favour, and thy visitation hath preserved my spirit." God gives life and favor. Both are gifts from God.

Unfortunately, there are multitudes of people who do not enjoy life. They are breathing but do not have life. Jesus came that we might have life, and life more abundantly. Favor is a part of the abundant life. Life without favor is hard and difficult.

Ridiculous favor will cause unusual manifestations of God's blessing in your life. You can live life in the overflow. You can have the abundant life. You can have miracles of breakthrough and provision in your life.

Chapter 3

FOUR WAYS TO FAVORED STATUS

Favor opens any door while it remains closed for everyone else.[1]

—Sunday Adelaja

WHAT IS YOUR status with the King? What is your relationship with Him? Are you now in favored status? Are your sins forgiven? Those who are in favored status can expect the favor of the King. In this chapter, we are going to look at four keys that put you in a favored status. Those keys are righteousness, humility, wisdom, and the presence of God.

1. RIGHTEOUSNESS—THE FOUNDATION OF FAVOR

When you have been declared righteous, when you're justified, when you're redeemed, when you're reconciled, you are put back in favored status with God. Your sins are washed and you have a relationship with God through Jesus Christ. Your righteousness is not based on you; it is based on Christ who is our righteousness.

Even those who feel they have lost favor can have favor restored. Through repentance and humility we can recover, and get back into favored status with the King.

> For thou, LORD, wilt bless the righteous; with favour
> wilt thou compass him as with a shield.
>
> —PSALM 5:12

You may say, "I am not righteous enough to receive God's favor. I have made mistakes. I am not satisfied with my growth and walk with the Lord." We all can improve in some area of our lives, but there is a righteousness that believers have that comes by faith. You are justified by faith. You are put in right standing with God through faith in Jesus Christ. Righteousness is one of the subjects that many believers don't fully understand. A revelation that you are the righteousness of God in Christ is indispensable if you want to walk in the favor of God.

> For he hath made him to be sin for us, who knew no sin;
> that we might be made the righteousness of God in him.
>
> —2 CORINTHIANS 5:21

Jesus was made to be sin, so that you could be made the righteousness of God in Him. This is an exchange. Jesus became sin; you become righteous.

> That God was in Christ reconciling the world to Himself,
> not counting people's sins against them [but canceling
> them]. And He has committed to us the message of rec-
> onciliation [that is, restoration to favor with God].
>
> —2 CORINTHIANS 5:19, AMP

Jesus died that we might be reconciled with God. *Reconcile* means "to restore to friendship or harmony."[2]

Reconciliation puts us back in right standing with God, which is the definition of righteousness. Reconciliation restores us to favor with God. Our repentance then Christ's forgiveness starts the process.

> Blessed and happy and favored are those whose lawless acts have been forgiven, and whose sins have been covered up and completely buried. Blessed and happy and favored is the man whose sin the Lord will not take into account nor charge against him.
>
> —ROMANS 4:7–8, AMP

This is the foundation of favor: We repent, Jesus brings forgiveness, we accept it, our sins are forgiven, and we are back in favor with God. The forgiven believer is the blessed and favored believer. Favor come to those whose sins are forgiven. Are your sins forgiven? If the answer is yes, then God remembers them no more. You are now in favored status.

> So then those who are people of faith [whether Jew or Gentile] are blessed and favored by God [and declared free of the guilt of sin and its penalty, and placed in right standing with Him] along with Abraham, the believer.
>
> —GALATIANS 3:9, AMP

Forgiveness and righteousness are received by faith. This faith begins to release the favor of God into our lives. Free from guilt, shame, and condemnation, we can now enjoy, confess, and walk in the favor of God, which is available to us by faith. Declare, "I am the righteousness of God." (See 2 Corinthians 5:21.)

Righteousness in Christ is the foundation upon which we begin to live a life of favor. We want to go from this foundation and then increase into ridiculous favor.

FAVOR MAGNETS

- Righteousness
- Glory
- Wisdom
- Giving
- Humility
- Understanding
- Knowledge
- Justice
- Seeking
- Faith
- Mercy
- Truth

2. HUMILITY—A KEY TO FAVOR

HUMILITY IS ABSOLUTELY necessary if you want to enjoy God's favor. God resists the proud, but shows grace, mercy, and favor to the humble. The humble man depends on the grace and favor of God. The humble man knows he cannot succeed without God's favor. The humble man recognizes his need for God's favor. While we all say that we want the favor of God, we need to examine ourselves to make sure we are not repelling the favor of God. In 1 Corinthians 1:26, the apostle Paul talks about three types of people who have difficulty receiving the favor of God: "For you see your calling, brethren, that not many wise according the flesh, not many mighty, not many noble are called."

1. The wise—those who are the highly educated
2. The mighty—those who are naturally talented
3. The noble—those who come from a privileged background

Minister Kong Hee says, "There is nothing at all wrong with any of these three social statuses. But one downfall that is common among the three is that these statuses often cause a higher dependence on 'self' and, as a result, an independence from God. And when we lose sight of our need for God in our lives, we shut the door from receiving His grace and favor."[3]

> I show special favor to the humble and contrite, who respect what I have to say.
>
> —ISAIAH 66:2, NET

I will look favorably on this kind of person: one who is humble, submissive in spirit, and trembles at my word.

—ISAIAH 66:2, CSB

For God sets Himself against the proud (the insolent, the overbearing, the disdainful, the presumptuous, the boastful)—[and He opposes, frustrates, and defeats them], but gives grace (favor, blessing) to the humble.

—1 PETER 5:5, HCSB

God opposes the arrogant but favors the humble.

—1 PETER 5:5, GW

Humble yourselves in the sight of the Lord, and he shall lift you up.

—JAMES 4:10

Pride will cause you to lose the favor of God. In the Bible we see examples of those who lost favor: Saul rebelled and lost favor. Israel rebelled and lost favor. Pride and rebellion will repel the favor of God from your life. God resists the proud (James 4:6).

> *Humility is the gateway into the grace and favor of God.[4]*
> *—Harold Warner*

Fasting leads to humility; humility leads to favor

Fasting has always been a way to seek the help of God during times of crisis, but it is also a way to attract the favor of God. Psalm 35:13 connects fasting with humility:

"But as for me, when they were sick, my clothing was sack-cloth: I humbled my soul with fasting; and my prayer returned into mine own bosom." You can humble your soul through fasting, and as your soul is humbled, you attract the favor of God. We also see humility attached to favor in Isaiah 58, where the Lord promises that great favor is released through fasting.

> Then shall thy light break forth as the morning, and thine health shall spring forth speedily: and thy righteousness shall go before thee; the glory of the LORD shall be thy reward.
>
> Then shalt thou call, and the LORD shall answer; thou shalt cry, and he shall say, Here I am. If thou take away from the midst of thee the yoke, the putting forth of the finger, and speaking vanity;
>
> —ISAIAH 58:8–9

> That thou appear not unto men to fast, but unto thy Father which is in secret: and thy Father, which seeth in secret, shall reward thee openly.
>
> —MATTHEW 6:18

Humility, submission, and favor

Many would not connect favor to submission, but they are related. Rebellion and antisubmissiveness is a sign of pride. Humility is connected to submission in that submission is a sign of humility. This also means that submission as a manifestation of humility is a key to favor. Let's look at three levels of submission that God requires.

1. Submit to God.

James 4:7 tells us that our first submission is to God: "Submit yourselves therefore to God. Resist the devil, and he will flee from you."

2. Submit to others.

In 1 Peter 5:5 we are also told to submit to one another: "Likewise, ye younger, submit yourselves unto the elder. Yea, all of you be subject one to another, and be clothed with humility: for God resisteth the proud, and giveth grace to the humble." This principle is a problem for many who claim submission to God only and are unable to submit appropriately to those around them.

This verse also shows that we are to be clothed (or covered) with humility. We should wear humility like a garment. As we humbly submit to one another, we attract the favor of God. (See Ephesians 5:21.)

Life is a long lesson in humility.[5]
—James M. Barrie

---

3. Submit to leaders.

Obey them that have the rule over you, and submit yourselves: for they watch for your souls, as they that must give account, that they may do it with joy, and not with grief: for that is unprofitable for you.

—HEBREWS 13:17

David was submitted to Saul. Joseph was submitted to Potiphar. Ruth submitted herself to Naomi. Daniel was submitted to the king. Esther submitted herself to Mordecai. Samuel was submitted to Eli. All these men and women of God received great favor, proving how important it is to honor the leadership God has placed within His body. God favors those who respect His servants and sent ones.

> He that receiveth a prophet in the name of a prophet shall receive a prophet's reward; and he that receiveth a righteous man in the name of a righteous man shall receive a righteous man's reward.
>
> —Matthew 10:41

God rewards and favors those who bless and favor His sent ones. Don't dishonor God's servants if you want His favor. I am not referring to controlling leaders, but leaders who walk in love and serve God's people.

When the favor of God is on you, good comes your way. Odds get turned in your favor.[6]
—Joseph Prince

In Philippians 4:19 Paul gave a promise to the Philippians after they supported and blessed his ministry. He told them, "My God shall supply all your need according to his riches in glory by Christ Jesus." You get favor when you bless men and women of God.

Luke 8:1–3 tells about the women who followed Jesus and ministered to them from their substance:

> And it came to pass afterward, that he went throughout every city and village, preaching and shewing the glad tidings of the kingdom of God: and the twelve were with him, and certain women, which had been healed of evil spirits and infirmities, Mary called Magdalene, out of whom went seven devils, and Joanna the wife of Chuza Herod's steward, and Susanna, and many others, which ministered unto him of their substance.

There is great favor when you bless those who have ministered to you and blessed you.

3. WISDOM—THE FAVOR MAGNET

Whoever finds wisdom finds life, and obtains favor from the Lord. (See Proverbs 8:35.) Wisdom is another key way to attract the King's favor. Joseph and Daniel were favored because of their wisdom and skill in interpreting dreams.

> The king's favour is toward a wise servant: but his wrath is against him that causeth shame.
>
> —PROVERBS 14:35

> Who then is a faithful and wise servant, whom his lord hath made ruler over his household, to give them meat in due season?
>
> —MATTHEW 24:45

A wise servant has the favor of the King. Are you a wise servant of the King? Do you steward the gifts that God has given you with wisdom? Is wisdom a part of your life and decisions? This is a key to receiving favor from the King.

There is no substitute for wisdom. If you were to ask, "What is the most important thing?" very few would answer, "Wisdom." But the Bible tells us that wisdom is the principal or primary thing you will need for success in life. (See Proverbs 4:7.)

> Wisdom is supreme—so get wisdom. And whatever else you get, get understanding.
>
> —CSB

> Wisdom is the most important thing.
>
> —EXB

Wisdom promises favor to those her receive her. Those who find wisdom are promised favor. Those who pursue wisdom and walk in wisdom will experience great favor. You cannot have ridiculous favor without wisdom. There are examples of this in Scripture. Joseph and Daniel had wisdom in interpreting dreams. They were both promoted and abstained favor. Solomon, the wisest of kings, received great favor. Solomon had ridiculous favor.

> And the speech pleased the LORD, that Solomon had asked this thing.
>
> And God said unto him, Because thou hast asked

this thing, and hast not asked for thyself long life; neither hast asked riches for thyself, nor hast asked the life of thine enemies; but hast asked for thyself understanding to discern judgment;

Behold, I have done according to thy words: lo, I have given thee a wise and an understanding heart; so that there was none like thee before thee, neither after thee shall any arise like unto thee.

—1 KINGS 3:10-12

Solomon was magnified exceedingly. This was the result of God's favor on his life.

And Solomon the son of David was strengthened in his kingdom, and the LORD his God was with him, and magnified him exceedingly.

—2 CHRONICLES 1:1

Solomon had favor with kings and queens. King Hiram gave Solomon cedar trees and fir trees according to all his desire (1 Kings 5:10). The queen of Sheba came to hear the wisdom of Solomon and brought a train of costly gifts to him. This is ridiculous favor. Solomon became the wealthiest and greatest king of his day.

And she came to Jerusalem with a very great train, with camels that bare spices, and very much gold, and precious stones: and when she was come to Solomon, she communed with him of all that was in her heart.

—1 KINGS 10:2

And she gave the king an hundred and twenty talents of gold, and of spices very great store, and precious stones: there came no more such abundance of spices as these which the queen of Sheba gave to king Solomon.

—1 Kings 10:10

And they brought every man his present, vessels of silver, and vessels of gold, and garments, and armour, and spices, horses, and mules, a rate year by year.

—1 Kings 10:25

Solomon was the most blessed man of his generation. Solomon received ridiculous favor.

And there came of all people to hear the wisdom of Solomon, from all kings of the earth, which had heard of his wisdom.

—1 Kings 4:34

Solomon was exalted and promoted because of God's favor. God also favored Solomon because of his covenant with David. God made Solomon famous. Solomon had ridiculous favor.

And when the queen of Sheba had seen all Solomon's wisdom, and the house that he had built, and the meat of his table, and the sitting of his servants, and the attendance of his ministers, and their apparel, and his cupbearers, and his ascent by which he went up unto the house of the LORD; there was no more spirit in her.

And she said to the king, It was a true report that I heard in mine own land of thy acts and of thy wisdom.

—1 KINGS 10:4–6

The queen of Sheba was amazed at the favor that was upon Solomon and his kingdom.

So king Solomon exceeded all the kings of the earth for riches and for wisdom.

—1 KINGS 10:23

For he was wiser than all men; than Ethan the Ezrahite, and Heman, and Chalcol, and Darda, the sons of Mahol: and his fame was in all nations round about.

—1 KINGS 4:31

And he spake three thousand proverbs: and his songs were a thousand and five.

—1 KINGS 4:32

Solomon lost this favor in his later years because he married strange women and worshipped strange gods. Pride gripped his heart, and he lost the favor that made him great. His kingdom was split after his death because of his disobedience.

Wisdom and the fear of God

The fear of the Lord is the beginning of wisdom. The fear of the Lord is therefore connected to favor.

Praise the LORD! (Hallelujah!) Blessed [fortunate, prosperous, and favored by God] is the man who fears the Lord [with awe-inspired reverence and worships Him with obedience], who delights greatly in His commandments.

—PSALM 112:1, AMP

The blessed, prosperous, and favored man is the man that fears the Lord with awe-inspired reverence. The Psalm 112 man is also the man who walks in wisdom and guides his affairs with discretion (verse 5).

Blessed [happy and sheltered by God's favor] is everyone who fears the LORD [and worships Him with obedience], who walks in His ways and lives according to His commandments.

—PSALM 128:1, AMP

Other biblical examples of wisdom and favor

- David had favor, and he was also wise. First Samuel 18:14 says, "And David behaved himself wisely in all his ways; and the LORD was with him."

- Joseph received favor from Pharaoh, and he was also wise: "And Pharaoh said unto Joseph, Forasmuch as God hath shewed thee all this, there is none so discreet and wise as thou art" (Gen. 41:39).

- Daniel was favored, and he was wise. Daniel's wisdom was ten times better than all the wise men of Babylon: "And in all matters of wisdom and understanding, that the king enquired of them, he found them ten times better than all the magicians and astrologers that were in all his realm" (Dan. 1:20).

+ Jesus increased in both favor and wisdom. We've discussed Luke 2:52 in a previous chapter, but I want to point out here that Jesus's increase in favor and wisdom indicates that an increase in wisdom will result in an increase of favor.

+ Abigail's wisdom saved her life, and gave her favor with David. Abigail becomes David's wife. (See 1 Samuel 25.)

+ Moses was favored, and he also had wisdom. Acts 7:22 says, "And Moses was learned in all the wisdom of the Egyptians, and was mighty in words and in deeds."

Wisdom includes prudence, discretion, knowledge, understanding, counsel, subtlety, and discernment. We need these things if we want to live a life of favor.

Wisdom and a crown of favor

Proverbs 4:9 tells us that wisdom will deliver to us a crown of favor. A crown is an ornament. An ornament is a thing used to make something look more attractive.

Favor makes you attractive. Favor cause people to be attracted to you.

> In that day shall the LORD of hosts be for a crown of glory, and for a diadem of beauty, unto the residue of his people.
>
> —ISAIAH 28:5

Favor releases a diadem of beauty. Beauty is connected to favor. We can have more favor as we walk in the beauty of holiness. Beauty is glory and majesty. Our God is a God of glory, beauty and majesty.

A crown is like a hat or turban, whereas the diadem is the most beautiful, glorious part of the crown. It is the headband. Generally speaking, a crown signifies glory, but its beauty is in its diadem, which may be full of jewels and precious stones. The diadem is the beauty of the glorious crown.

> And let the beauty of the LORD our God be upon us: and establish thou the work of our hands upon us; yea, the work of our hands establish thou it.
>
> —PSALM 90:17

> O worship the LORD in the beauty of holiness: fear before him, all the earth.
>
> —PSALM 96:9

To be crowned with favor means to be under God's favor. The crown sits on the head. What is on the head flows down to the rest of the body. The crown also represents power and authority. Favor will promote you and bring you to a place of power and authority. Favor can bring you to a place of glory and honor.

> Who redeemeth thy life from destruction; who crowneth thee with lovingkindness and tender mercies.
>
> —PSALM 103:4

> He forgives your sins—every one. He heals your diseases—every one. He redeems you from hell—saves your life! He crowns you with love and mercy—a paradise crown. He wraps you in goodness—beauty eternal. He renews your youth—you're always young in his presence.
>
> —PSALM 103:3–5, THE MESSAGE

Lovingkindness is favor and grace. God crowns you with lovingkindness and tender mercies.

> For thou preventest him with the blessings of goodness: thou settest a crown of pure gold on his head.
>
> —PSALM 21:3

David the king received the blessings of goodness. God put a crown of pure gold on his head. David walked in the favor of God.

4. THE PRESENCE OF GOD—THE FAVOR REALM

The presence of God houses the glory of God. The glory realm is the realm of worship. The glory realm is the realm of light, majesty, and beauty. God's glory brings strength and favor. Favor will cause your horn to be exalted. In this we find that favor and glory are connected.

> For the Lord GOD is a sun and shield; the LORD will give favor and glory, for no good thing will He withhold from the one who walks uprightly.
>
> —PSALM 84:11, MEV

> For thou art the glory of their strength: and in thy favour our horn shall be exalted.
>
> —PSALM 89:17

Isaiah 60 is the glory chapter and the prophecy revealed in this chapter includes declarations of promotion, wealth, favor, increase, restoration, and light.

> Foreigners will build up your walls, and their kings will serve you; for in My [righteous] wrath I struck you, but in My favor and grace I have had compassion on you.
>
> —ISAIAH 60:10

Favor will cause foreigners and strangers to bless you. Favor will cause abundance to come into your life.

> Then thou shall see, and flow together, and shine heart shall fear, and be enlarged; because the abundance of the sea shall be converted unto thee, the forces of the Gentiles shall come unto thee.
>
> —ISAIAH 60:4

In Hebrew, the word for *forces* in this verse is translated as "wealth." Wealth is associated or connected to favor.

Isaiah chapter 60 goes on to speak of the great things that come upon God's people as a result of His glory. Favor is released when glory comes. Our churches and assemblies should be filled with the glory and presence of God. Worship is designed to be a glory encounter where we can be positioned to receive the King's favor.

Glory is power.
   Glory is weight.
Glory is honor.
   Glory is great.

Glory is favor.
   Glory is strength.
Glory is excellence.
   Glory is wealth.

Glory will attract
   The riches you need,
Glory will impress
   Those who will see.

Glory is beauty.
   Glory is light.
Glory is brilliance.
   It shines in the night.

Glory brings kings.
   They come from afar.
Glory brings nations.
   Glory shines like a star.

God has put
  His glory in you,
His glory will cause.
  You to breakthrough.

Arise and shine,
  For your light has come.
The glory of the Lord
  Has risen upon you.

Glory in the Bible means splendor, light, majesty, shining, power, fame, wealth, abundance, riches, goodness, mercy, beauty, might, excellence, favor, praise, renown, weight, importance, attractiveness. It means God's manifest presence—Shekinah. It also means cloud, fire, shining, brightness, protection. Glory is the presence of God that attracts His favor.

Chapter 4

SIMPLY ASK

Ask, and it shall be given you; seek, and ye shall find; knock, and it shall be opened unto you: for every one that asketh receiveth; and he that seeketh findeth; and to him that knocketh it shall be opened. Or what man is there of you, whom if his son ask bread, will he give him a stone?

—MATTHEW 7:7–9

A S SIMPLE AS it seems, asking for favor is another way to receive favor. God encourages us to ask. Asking shows humility, because only those who recognize their need for favor will ask for it. Ephesians 3:20 tells us that God is able to do exceeding abundantly above all that we can ask or think. The Lord invites us to seek His favor. (See Psalm 119:58, 135; 2 Kings 13:4; Jeremiah 26:19.)

In Psalm 119:58 the psalmist sought God's favor: "I entreated thy favour with my whole heart: be merciful unto me according to thy word." To *entreat* means to make an earnest request. In the Amplified Bible version, this verse reads, "I sought Your favor with all my heart; Be merciful and gracious to me according to Your promise." The International Children's Bible translates it this way: "I prayed to you with all my heart. Be kind to me as you have promised."

Favor can result in a greater understanding of God's

word: "Show favor to Your servant, and teach me Your statutes" (Ps. 119:135, HCSB).

Favor will help deliver and set you free. In 2 Kings 13:4 Jehoahaz received deliverance by seeking God's favor: "But Jehoahaz sought the favor of the LORD, and the LORD listened to him; for He saw the oppression of Israel, how the king of Aram oppressed them" (AMP).

> Seek the LORD's favor, all you humble people of the land who have obeyed his commands! Strive to do what is right! Strive to be humble! Maybe you will be protected on the day of the Lord's angry judgment.
>
> —ZEPHANIAH 2:3, NET

One day of favor is worth a
thousand days of labor.
—Unknown

The throne of grace is a throne of favor. Don't be afraid to ask for favor. We all need favor. Some have not because they ask not.

> Let us therefore come boldly unto the throne of grace, that we may obtain mercy, and find grace to help in time of need.
>
> —HEBREWS 4:16

Finally, let's draw near to the throne of favor with confidence so that we can receive mercy and find grace when we need help.

—HEBREWS 4:16, CEB

You can ask for favor with confidence. You can ask knowing that God is willing and ready to answer you.

Therefore let us [with privilege] approach the throne of grace [that is, the throne of God's gracious favor] with confidence and without fear, so that we may receive mercy [for our failures] and find [His amazing] grace to help in time of need [an appropriate blessing, coming just at the right moment].

—HEBREWS 4:16, AMP

We are encouraged to come boldly to the throne of grace with our requests. Do you need grace? Do you need favor? You can find grace and favor in the time of need by asking for it. We can come bold. We don't have to be afraid. God will not correct or rebuke you for asking. You have the privilege of asking God for grace and favor. This is your covenant right as a child of God.

ASK AND KEEP ASKING

In her book *The Anna Anointing*, Michelle McClain-Walters looks at the life and anointing of the prophetess Anna. She says that Anna's name means "grace." She goes on to say that "her name comes from a root word meaning 'to grant a favor, to be gracious, and to favor' or 'we beseech thee!'" McClain-Walters brings to light that "the word *beseech* paints the picture of a person earnestly praying. It means 'to beg for urgently or anxiously; to request earnestly; to make supplication.'" She goes on to say this:

> Anna's name speaks of both grace and supplication. The modern-day Anna will find favor in the presence of the Lord. She will have favor with God and favor with men. Built into the DNA of those with an Anna anointing is an ability to beseech the Lord with fervency and zeal of intercession. Because they have spent time abiding in the presence of the Lord, they will ask what they will and it shall be given. Those with an Anna anointing will sincerely offer compassionate intercession that moves the heart and hand of God. They will have grace to beseech the Lord to release His mercy and kindness. They will be empowered by the spirit of grace and supplication.[1]

God's favor will turn everything around.[2]
—Judy Jacobs

Will you be like Anna and earnestly pray for the favor of God to come upon your life? It is not a one-time asking. Favor is for a lifetime and in humility, you know you cannot live without the favor of God. Several other biblical examples reveal how the people of God relentlessly sought after ridiculous favor.

The people of Bethel

In seeking God's favor, "the people of Bethel had sent Sharezer and Regemmelech, along with their attendants, to seek the LORD's favor" (Zech. 7:2, NLT). Scholars say that this act of going before the Lord literally was like stroking "the face of the LORD (Zechariah 8:21–22; Exodus 32:11); so Latin, *mulcere caput*. Hence it means, "to entreat the favour of God" for their city. This was one object of their mission."[3]

Jabez

Jabez asked for God's blessing and favor. God granted him that he requested. God did it for Jabez, and he will do it for you.

> And Jabez called on the God of Israel, saying, Oh that thou wouldest bless me indeed, and enlarge my coast, and that thine hand might be with me, and that thou wouldest keep me from evil, that it may not grieve me! And God granted him that which he requested.
>
> —1 CHRONICLES 4:10

If you ask for favor, you will receive favor. Favor is available. You must desire it, ask for it, and seek it.

> And all things, whatsoever ye shall ask in prayer, believing, ye shall receive.
>
> —MATTHEW 21:22

Ask in faith. Believe that you receive favor when you ask. Don't doubt God's lovingkindness and desire to give you His favor.

> And let the favor of the LORD our God be upon us; and establish thou the work of our hands upon us; yea, the work of our hands establish thou it.
>
> —PSALM 90:17, ASV

GOD LAVISHES HIS FAVOR ON THOSE WHO ASK

To *lavish* means to bestow something in generous or extravagant quantities.

> Generous to a fault, you lavish your favor on all creatures.
>
> —PSALM 145:16, THE MESSAGE

God is generous. God gives liberally. God is gracious. God is rich in favor.

> Then the LORD passed by in front of him, saying, "The LORD, the Lord GOD, with loving-pity and loving-favor, slow to anger, filled with loving-kindness and truth."
>
> —EXODUS 34:6, NLV

God is rich in grace. He is rich in favor. He possesses more than enough to bless all of His people.

> In whom we have—redemption through his blood, the forgiveness of sins, according to the riches of his grace.
>
> —EPHESIANS 1:7

In Him we have redemption (deliverance and salvation) through His blood, the remission (forgiveness) of our offenses (shortcomings and trespasses), in accordance with the riches and the generosity of His gracious favor.

— Ephesians 1:7, ampc

The riches of His grace are the riches of His favor. We can experience these riches in Christ.

If any of you lack wisdom, let him ask of God, that giveth to all men liberally, and upbraideth not; and it shall be given him.

—James 1:5

If any of you lacks wisdom [to guide him through a decision or circumstance], he is to ask of [our benevolent] God, who gives to everyone generously and without rebuke or blame, and it will be given to him.

—James 1:5, amp

[No one] for there is no distinction between Jew and Greek. The same Lord is Lord over all [of us] and He generously bestows His riches upon all who call upon Him [in faith].

—Romans 10:12, ampc

God pours out His favor and blessing. His downpour is likened to a flood. Ridiculous favor is a flood of favor. Our cup will run over with favor (Ps. 23:5). Our lives will be so full of favor that there will not be room enough to receive it (Mal. 3:10).

Grace and favor are multiplied through the correct knowledge of God. Growing in knowledge will increase the flow of favor into our lives. Second Peter 1:2 says, "May grace (God's favor) and peace (which is perfect well-being, all necessary good, all spiritual prosperity, and freedom from fears and agitating passions and moral conflicts) be multiplied to you in [the full, personal, precise, and correct] knowledge of God and of Jesus our Lord" (AMPC).

> But let him that glorieth glory in this, that he understandeth and knoweth me, that I am the LORD which exercise lovingkindness, judgment, and righteousness, in the earth: for in these things I delight, saith the LORD.
> —JEREMIAH 9:24

There are many scriptures that stress the importance of knowledge. We gain knowledge by studying God's Word. We gain knowledge by listening to teachers. The knowledge of God is necessary if you want to enjoy His favor.

> For the earth shall be filled with the knowledge of the glory of the LORD, as the waters cover the sea.
> —HABAKKUK 2:14

ASK FOR FAVOR FOR YOUR LEADERS

Intercession is another powerful way to release God's favor. We should pray for our leaders to receive favor. Pray for your pastors to receive favor. Leaders need favor to complete their assignments. Here are some points to add to your prayers for your leaders.

- Pray for favor for your pastor with the community.
- Pray for favor for your pastor with the city and city officials.
- Pray for favor for your pastor for open doors to preach the gospel.
- Pray for favor for your pastor with other ministries in the city.
- Pray for favor for your pastor for land and property.
- Pray for favor for your pastor with zoning boards and license boards.
- Pray for favor for your pastor for increase and growth for the ministry.
- Pray for favor for your pastor for finances.
- Pray for favor for your pastor for open doors in ministry.
- Pray for favor for your pastor with media.
- Pray for favor for your pastor for divine connections with the right people.
- Pray for your pastor's family to have favor.
- Pray for favor for your pastor for transportation.

- Pray for favor for your pastor for venues and buildings.
- Pray for favor for your pastor in networking with other ministries.
- Pray for favor for your pastor for the right platforms for ministry.
- Pray for favor for your pastor with businesses.
- Pray for favor for your pastor with architects.
- Pray for favor for your pastor with equipment.

Ye also helped by praying together for us, so that for the gift bestowed upon us by means of many persons, thanks may be given by many on our behalf.

—2 Corinthians 1:11

...you also joining in helping us through your prayers, so that thanks may be given by many persons on our behalf for the favor bestowed on us through the prayers of many.

—NAS

...as you also help us by your prayers for us. Then many people will thank God on our behalf because of the favor shown us through the prayers of many.

—ISV

Chapter 5

BENEDICTIONS, PRAYERS, AND DECREES THAT RELEASE FAVOR

Let the [gracious] favor of the LORD our God be on us; confirm for us the work of our hands—yes, confirm the work of our hands.

—PSALM 90:17, AMP

AVOR AND BLESSINGS are connected. Favor can be released through spoken benedictions and blessings. A benediction is the invocation of a blessing. It is a spoken blessing over people. The priests of Israel were told to speak this blessing over Israel. God promised to bless them as a result. This benediction asks for God's favor:

> The LORD make his face shine upon thee, and be gracious unto thee: the LORD lift up his countenance upon thee, and give thee peace. And they shall put my name upon the children of Israel, and I will bless them.
>
> —NUMBERS 6:25–27

> The LORD make His face shine upon you [with favor], And be gracious to you [surrounding you with lovingkindness].
>
> —NUMBERS 6:25, AMP

Paul spoke a blessing of favor over the churches.

The grace of our Lord Jesus Christ be with you.
> —1 CORINTHIANS 16:23

The grace (favor and spiritual blessing) of our Lord Jesus
Christ be with you.
> —1 CORINTHIANS 16:23, AMPC

I also bless the congregation at the conclusion of our
services. I encourage people to remain for the benediction. Benedictions by those with spiritual authority are
powerful.

Moses blessed the tribes of Israel before his death. He
spoke a word of favor over several of the tribes. He spoke
a word of favor over the tribe of Naphtali.

And of Naphtali he said, O Naphtali, satisfied with
favour, and full with the blessing of the LORD: possess
thou the west and the south.
> —DEUTERONOMY 33:23

This favor would result in Naphtali possessing the
west and the south. Favor can help you possess land and
acquire real estate.

> One touch of His [God's] favor can put you fifty
> years ahead of where you thought you'd be.[1]
> —Joel Osteen

Moses also spoke a word of favor and goodwill over
the head of Joseph (Manasseh and Ephraim): "With
the precious things of the earth and its fullness, and the

favor and goodwill of Him who dwelt in the bush. Let these blessings come upon the head of Joseph, and upon the crown of the head of him who was distinguished [as a prince] among his brothers" (Deut. 33:16, AMP).

Favor can be prophesied over someone's life. Prophets and prophetic people can speak a word of favor over your life. The prophetic word can release you into a realm of ridiculous favor.

WIND OF FAVOR PROPHECY

There is strong wind of favor that is about to blow over those who believe the Lord our God and the prophets of God. Those who believe in the Lord will be established; those who believe in His prophets will prosper. Surely, there is a mighty rushing wind of favor blowing.

The winds of God are about to blow over your life. "Prophesy to the four winds as I told Ezekiel, and I will breathe new life into to your dreams and visions," says the Lord. "Your enemies have tried to kill your dreams and visions, but I am dealing with dream killers and I am resuscitating and reawakening your dream and visions with My fresh wind. My wind of deliverance is blowing to deliver you from the opinions of man and release you out your bondage. I'm about to breathe on you. I'm about to blow on your life and you will feel My favor. I command My winds of favor to blow on you! My winds of favor are blowing," says God, "and the things you could not do in the past, My favor will do for you in the days ahead.

"My winds of favor are here to refresh you. This wind of favor is a wind of change. This wind of favor is a wind that will transform your life.

"This wind is about to orchestrate new opportunities for you and new open doors for you. Yes, this wind of favor will open new doors for you, and no man can shut these doors. New moments of favor are coming upon you because winds of favor are surrounding you."[2]

—Michelle J. Miller

There are other blessings in Scripture. Remember grace also means favor.

Biblical Blessings That Release Grace

To all that be in Rome, beloved of God, called to be saints: Grace to you and peace from God our Father, and the Lord Jesus Christ.

—Romans 1:7

Peace to the brothers, and love with faith from God the Father and the Lord Jesus Christ. Grace to all who love our Lord Jesus Christ with an undying love."

—Ephesians 6:23–24

Grace, mercy and peace from God the Father and Christ Jesus our Lord.

—1 Timothy 1:2

Grace and peace be yours in abundance, through the knowledge of God and of Jesus our Lord.

—2 PETER 1:2

PRAYERS FOR BLESSING AND FAVOR

Lord, bless me and keep me. Make Your face to shine upon me, and be gracious unto me. Lord, lift up Your countenance upon me and give me peace (Num. 6:24–26).

Make me as Ephraim and Manasseh (Gen. 48:20).

Let me be satisfied with favor and filled with Your blessing (Deut. 33:23).

Lord, command Your blessing upon my life.

Give me revelation, and let me be blessed (Matt. 16:17).

I am the seed of Abraham through Jesus Christ, and I receive the blessing of Abraham. Lord, in blessing, bless me, and in multiplying, multiply me as the stars of heaven and as the sand of the seashore.

Let Your showers of blessing be upon my life (Ezek. 34:26).

Turn every curse sent my way into a blessing (Neh. 13:2).

Let Your blessing make me rich (Prov. 10:22).

Let all nations call me blessed (Mal. 3:12).

Let all generations call me blessed (Luke 1:48).

I am a son of the blessed (Mark 14:61).

I live in the kingdom of the blessed (Mark 11:10).

My sins are forgiven, and I am blessed (Rom. 4:7).

Lord, You daily load me with benefits (Ps. 68:19).

I am chosen by God, and I am blessed (Ps. 65:4).

My seed is blessed (Ps. 37:26).

Let me inherit the land (Ps. 37:22).

I am a part of a holy nation, and I am blessed (Ps. 33:12).

Lord, bless my latter end more than my beginning (Job 42:12).

Lord, let Your presence bless my life (2 Sam. 6:11).

I drink the cup of blessing (1 Cor. 10:16).

Lord, bless me, and cause Your face to shine upon me, that Your way may be known upon the earth and Your saving health among all nations. Let my land yield increase, and let the ends of the earth fear You (Ps. 67).

I know You favor me because my enemies do not triumph over me (Ps. 41:11).

Lord, be favorable unto my land (Ps. 85:1).

Lord, grant me life and favor (Job 10:12).

In Your favor, Lord, make my mountain stand strong (Ps. 30:7).

Lord, I entreat Your favor (Ps. 45:12).

Let Your favor cause my horn to be exalted (Ps. 89:17).

Lord, this is my set time for favor (Ps. 102:13).

Remember me, O Lord, with the favor that You bring unto Your children, and visit me with Your salvation (Ps. 106:4).

Lord, I entreat Your favor with my whole heart (Ps. 119:58).

Let Your favor be upon my life as a cloud of the latter rain (Prov. 16:15).

Let Your beauty be upon my life, and let me be well favored (Gen. 29:17).

I am highly favored (Luke 1:28).

Lord, let me receive extraordinary favor.

FAVOR DECREE AND CONFESSIONS

I believe in Jesus. I confess Him as my Lord. I am justified by faith. I have been declared righteous. I am the righteousness of God in Christ. I have been reconciled. I am back in favored status with God.

I am increasing in favor with God and man. I humble myself and receive more favor and grace in my life.

I come boldly to the throne of favor. I obtain mercy and favor in the time of need. I ask You Lord for favor.

I am increasing in wisdom, knowledge and understanding, and I am increasing in favor.

I am a giver, and I enjoy favor. God makes all favor abound in my life, and I have sufficiency in all things.

My gifts make room for me and bring me before great men (Prov. 18:16). I have favor with influential and powerful people.

Every curse against me is turned into a blessing because of favor.

Favor attracts wealth and riches and brings them into my life.

Favor brings the right people into my life.

Favor causes bills to be decreased and paid off.

Favor causes me to lend and not borrow.

Favor causes me to be enlarged.

Favor causes me to break limitations.

Favor causes me to enjoy the best.

Favor causes me to see what others miss.

Favor causes me to succeed where others fail.

Favor causes people to bless me.

Favor causes people to help and assist me.

Favor enables me to overcome opposition.

Favor expands my borders.

Favor floods my life.

Favor flows out of my life like a river.

Favor follows me wherever I go.

Favor follows me.

Favor gives me bonuses and bonanza.

RIDICULOUS FAVOR

Favor gives me discounts and dividends.

Favor gives me gifts and surprises.

Favor gives me multiplied victories.

Favor gives me new opportunities.

Favor gives me second chances.

Favor is multiplied in my life.

Favor is my portion in life.

Favor is poured from heaven upon my life.

Favor lifts me above my enemies.

Favor locates me wherever I go.

Favor makes difficult things easy for me.

Favor makes me above and not beneath.

Favor makes me the head and not the tail.

Favor makes my mountain strong.

Favor makes my way prosperous.

Favor makes the impossible possible for me.

Favor opens doors for me.

Favor paves the way for my success.

Favor promotes me.

Favor surrounds me like a shield.

Favors causes me to go where others cannot go.

God causes things to work in my favor.

God has marked me for favor.

God's favor falls on me like rain.

I always increase in favor.

I am a recipient of the King's favor.

I am clothed in favor.

I am covered by the flood of favor.

I am highly favored.

I am impacted by the winds of favor.

I am one of God's favorites.

I am overwhelmed by an avalanche of favor.

I am refreshed by the dew of favor.

I am revived by the breath of favor.

I am rich with favor.

I am soaked in the rain of favor.

RIDICULOUS FAVOR

I am surrounded by favor.

I ask and receive wisdom and favor.

I associate with those who are favored.

I come to the throne of favor.

I confess and receive a crown of favor

I confess and receive a free flow of favor.

I confess and receive an abundance of favor.

I confess and receive an anointing for favor.

I confess and receive an avalanche of favor.

I confess and receive extraordinary favor.

I confess and receive favor with influential people.

I confess and receive heaps of favor.

I confess and receive mega favor.

I confess and receive ridiculous favor.

I confess and receive special favor.

I confess and receive the King's favor.

I confess and receive unusual favor.

I confess favor for today and the future.

I draw from the well of favor.

I drink from the fountain of favor.

I enjoy a lifetime of favor.

I enjoy extreme favor.

I enjoy financial favor.

I enjoy new favor.

I go from favor to favor.

I harvest from the field of favor.

I have a banner of favor over my life.

I have a lifetime of favor.

I have an abundance of favor.

I have an angel of favor.

I have an anointing for favor.

I have favor for breakthroughs.

I have favor for health and prosperity.

I have favor for thousands and ten thousands.

I have favor in my city.

I have favor with God and man.

RIDICULOUS FAVOR

I have financial favor.

I have gifts that bring favor.

I have strong faith for favor.

I have the dew of favor on my life.

I live by the river of favor.

I live in a new season of favor.

I live under a cloud of favor.

I live with unusual favor.

I obtain ridiculous favor.

I praise the Lord for favor.

I reap heaps of favor.

I receive a downpour of favor.

I receive favorable reports.

I receive gifts and grants through favor.

I receive the word of favor.

I release my faith for favor.

I sow favor, and I reap a harvest of favor.

I understand favor.

I walk in divine favor.

I walk in extraordinary favor.

I walk in the path of favor.

I walk in the revelation of favor.

I wear the coat of favor.

I wear the crown of favor.

I will never lack favor.

I will sing about favor.

I will walk in mercy and truth, and I will walk in favor.

Let the river of favor flow into my life.

My career is favored.

My cup runs over with favor.

My ideas are favored.

My life overruns with favor.

My projects are favored.

My relationships are favored.

My steps are favored of the Lord.

The glory of God is upon me, and I enjoy His favor.

RIDICULOUS FAVOR

The wealth of the wicked comes into my hand because of favor.

The winds of favor blow in my life.

This is a set time of favor for my life.

Time and chance work in my favor.

What the enemy meant for evil works in my favor.

Wisdom gives me favor.

Part 2

FAVOR IN THE WORD

Chapter 6

FAVOR IN THE OLD TESTAMENT

GENESIS

But Noah found favor and grace in the eyes of the LORD.

—GENESIS 6:8, AMP

Melchizedek blessed Abram and said, "Blessed (joyful, favored) be Abram by God Most High, Creator and Possessor of heaven and earth."

—GENESIS 14:19, AMP

My LORD, if now I have found favour in thy sight, pass not away, I pray thee, from thy servant:

—GENESIS 18:3

Please listen, your servant has found favor in your sight, and you have magnified your lovingkindness (mercy) to me by saving my life; but I cannot escape to the mountains, because the disaster will overtake me and I will be killed.

—GENESIS 19:19, AMP

Now Isaac loved [and favored] Esau, because he enjoyed eating his game, but Rebekah loved [and favored] Jacob.

—GENESIS 25:28, AMP

Live temporarily [as a resident] in this land and I will be with you and will bless and favor you, for I will give all these lands to you and to your descendants, and I

69

will establish and carry out the oath which I swore to Abraham your father.

—GENESIS 26:3, AMP

Then Isaac planted [seed] in that land [as a farmer] and reaped in the same year a hundred times [as much as he had planted], and the LORD blessed and favored him.

—GENESIS 26:12, AMP

The LORD appeared to him the same night and said, "I am the God of Abraham your father; do not be afraid, for I am with you. I will bless and favor you, and multiply your descendants, for the sake of My servant Abraham."

—GENESIS 26:24, AMP

There should now be an oath between us [with a curse for the one who breaks it], that is, between you and us, and let us make a covenant (binding agreement, solemn promise) with you, that you will not harm us, just as we have not touched you and have done nothing but good to you and have sent you away in peace. You are now the blessed and favored of the LORD!

—GENESIS 26:28–29, AMP

Now when Isaac was old and his eyes were too dim to see, he called his elder [and favorite] son Esau and said to him, "My son." And Esau answered him, "Here I am."

—GENESIS 27:1, AMP

For you had little before I came and it has increased and multiplied abundantly, and the LORD has favored you with blessings wherever I turned. But now, when shall I provide for my own household?"

—GENESIS 30:30, AMP

Early in the morning Laban got up and kissed his grandchildren and his daughters [goodbye] and pronounced a blessing [asking God's favor] on them. Then Laban left and returned home.

—GENESIS 31:55, AMP

Leah was tender eyed; but Rachel was beautiful and well favoured.

—GENESIS 29:17

And Laban said unto him, I pray thee, if I have found favour in thine eyes, tarry: for I have learned by experience that the LORD hath blessed me for thy sake.

—GENESIS 30:27

And he left all that he had in Joseph's hand; and he knew not ought he had, save the bread which he did eat. And Joseph was a goodly person, and well favoured.

—GENESIS 39:6

But the LORD was with Joseph, and shewed him mercy, and gave him favour in the sight of the keeper of the prison.

—GENESIS 39:21

And, behold, there came up out of the river seven well favoured kine and fatfleshed; and they fed in a meadow. And, behold, seven other kine came up after them out of the river, ill favoured and leanfleshed; and stood by the other kine upon the brink of the river. And the ill favoured and leanfleshed kine did eat up the seven well favoured and fat kine. So Pharaoh awoke.

—GENESIS 41:2–4

And, behold, there came up out of the river seven kine, fatfleshed and well favoured; and they fed in a meadow: and, behold, seven other kine came up after them, poor and very ill favoured and leanfleshed, such as I never saw in all the land of Egypt for badness: and the lean and the ill favoured kine did eat up the first seven fat kine: and when they had eaten them up, it could not be known that they had eaten them; but they were still ill favored, as at the beginning. So I awoke.

—GENESIS 41:18–21

And the seven thin and ill favoured kind that came up after them are seven years; and the seven empty ears blasted with the east wind shall be seven years of famine.

—GENESIS 41:27

EXODUS

And I will give this people favor in the sight of the Egyptians: and it shall come to pass, that, when ye go, ye shall not go empty.

—Exodus 3:21

And the LORD gave the people favour in the sight of the Egyptians, so that they lent unto them such things as they required. And they spoiled the Egyptians.

—Exodus 12:36

Nor shall you favor or be partial to a poor man in his dispute [simply because he is poor].

—Exodus 23:3, AMP

The LORD said to Moses, "I will also do this thing that you have asked; for you have found favor (lovingkindness, mercy) in My sight and I have known you [personally] by name."

—Exodus 33:17, AMP

LEVITICUS

For I will turn toward you [with favor and regard] and make you fruitful and multiply you, and I will establish and confirm My covenant with you.

—Leviticus 26:9, AMP

NUMBERS

Then the man shall bring his wife to the priest, and he shall bring as an offering for her, a tenth of an ephah of barley meal; he shall not pour oil on it nor put frankincense on it [the symbols of favor and joy], because it is a grain offering of jealousy, a memorial grain offering, a reminder of [the consequences of] wickedness.

—NUMBERS 5:15, AMP

The LORD make His face shine upon you [with favor], and be gracious to you [surrounding you with lovingkindness].

—NUMBERS 6:25, AMP

And Moses said unto the LORD, Wherefore hast thou afflicted thy servant? and wherefore have I not found favor in thy sight, that thou layest the burden of all this people upon me?

—NUMBERS 11:11

And if thou deal thus with me, kill me, I pray thee, out of hand, if I have found favor in thy sight; and let me not see my wretchedness.

—NUMBERS 11:15

They said, "If we have found favor in your sight, let this land be given to your servants as a possession. Do not take us across the Jordan [River]."

—NUMBERS 32:5, AMP

DEUTERONOMY

Then I pleaded with the LORD at that time [for His favor], saying, "O Lord GOD, You have only begun to show Your servant Your greatness and Your mighty hand; for what god is there in heaven or on earth that can do such works and mighty acts (miracles) as Yours?"

—DEUTERONOMY 3:23–24, AMP

When a man hath taken a wife, and married her, and it come to pass that she find no favour in his eyes, because he hath found some uncleanness in her: then let him write her a bill of divorcement, and give it in her hand, and send her out of his house.

—DEUTERONOMY 24:1

If there is a controversy between men, and they go to court, and the judges decide [the issue] between them, and they judge in favor of the innocent and condemn the guilty.

—DEUTERONOMY 25:1, AMP

A nation of fierce countenance, which shall not regard the person of the old, nor shew favour to the young:

—DEUTERONOMY 28:50

With the precious things of the earth and its fullness, And the favor and goodwill of Him who dwelt in the bush. Let these blessings come upon the head of Joseph, and upon the crown of the head of him who was distinguished [as a prince] among his brothers.

—DEUTERONOMY 33:16, AMP

And of Naphtali he said, O Naphtali, satisfied with favor, and full with the blessing of the LORD: possess thou the west and the south.

—DEUTERONOMY 33:23

JOSHUA

For it was of the Lord to harden their hearts, that they should come against Israel in battle, that he might destroy them utterly, and that they might have no favor, but that he might destroy them, as the Lord commanded Moses.

—JOSHUA 11:20

JUDGES

Then Micah said, "Now I know that the Lord will favor me and make me prosper because I have a Levite as my priest."

—JUDGES 17:13, AMP

And it shall be, when their fathers or their brethren come unto us to complain, that we will say unto them, Be favourable unto them for our sakes: because we reserved not to each man his wife in the war: for ye did not give unto them at this time, that ye should be guilty.

—JUDGES 21:22

Ruth

Then she said, Let me find favor in thy sight, my lord; for that thou hast comforted me, and for that thou hast spoken friendly unto thine handmaid, though I be not like unto one of thine handmaidens.

—Ruth 2:13

1 Samuel

And the child Samuel grew on, and was in favor both with the Lord, and also with men.

—1 Samuel 2:26

Therefore, I said, "Now the Philistines will come down against me at Gilgal, and I have not asked for the Lord's favor [by making supplication to Him]." So I forced myself to offer the burnt offering.

—1 Samuel 13:12, amp

And Saul sent to Jesse, saying, Let David, I pray thee, stand before me; for he hath found favor in my sight.

—1 Samuel 16:22

But David vowed again, saying "Your father certainly knows that I have found favor in your sight, and he has said, 'Do not let Jonathan know this, or he will be worried.' But truly as the Lord lives and as your soul lives, there is hardly a step between me and death."

—1 Samuel 20:3, amp

And he said, Let me go, I pray thee; for our family hath a sacrifice in the city; and my brother, he hath commanded me to be there: and now, if I have found favor in thine eyes, let me get away, I pray thee, and see my brethren. Therefore he cometh not unto the king's table.

—1 SAMUEL 20:29

Ask thy young men, and they will shew thee. Wherefore let the young men find favor in thine eyes: for we come in a good day: give, I pray thee, whatsoever cometh to thine hand unto thy servants, and to thy son David.

—1 SAMUEL 25:8

…that this [incident] will not cause grief or [bring] a troubled conscience to my lord, both by having shed blood without cause and by my lord having avenged himself. When the LORD deals well with my lord, then remember [with favor] your maidservant.

—1 SAMUEL 25:31, AMP

Then Achish called David, and said unto him, Surely, as the LORD liveth, thou hast been upright, and thy going out and thy coming in with me in the host is good in my sight: for I have not found evil in thee since the day of thy coming unto me unto this day: nevertheless the lords favor thee not.

—1 SAMUEL 29:6

And the king said unto Zadok, Carry back the ark of God into the city: if I shall find favor in the eyes of the

Lord, he will bring me again, and shew me both it, and his habitation.

—2 Samuel 15:25

And one of Joab's men stood by him, and said, He that favoreth Joab, and he that is for David, let him go after Joab.

—2 Samuel 20:11

1 Kings

My servants will bring the logs down from Lebanon to the [Mediterranean] sea, and I will have them made into rafts to go by sea to the place (port) that you direct me; then I will have them broken up there, and you shall carry them away. Then you shall return the favor by providing food for my household.

—1 Kings 5:9, amp

When Your people Israel are defeated before an enemy because they have sinned against You, and then they turn to You again and praise Your Name and pray and ask for Your favor and compassion in this house (temple).

—1 Kings 8:33, amp

And Hadad found great favor in the sight of Pharaoh, so that he gave him to wife the sister of his own wife, the sister of Tahpenes the queen.

—1 Kings 11:19

The king answered and said to the man of God, "Please entreat [the favor of] the Lord your God and pray for me, that my hand may be restored to me." So the man of God entreated the LORD, and the king's hand was restored to him and became as it was before.

—1 KINGS 13:6, AMP

2 KINGS

But Jehoahaz sought the favor of the LORD, and the LORD listened to him; for He saw the oppression of Israel, how the king of Aram oppressed them.

—2 KINGS 13:4, AMP

NEHEMIAH

And I said unto the king, If it please the king, and if thy servant have found favour in thy sight, that thou wouldest send me unto Judah, unto the city of my fathers' sepulchres, that I may build it.

—NEHEMIAH 2:5

ESTHER

So it came about when the king's command and his decree were proclaimed and when many young women were gathered together in the citadel of Susa into the custody of Hegai, that Esther was taken to the king's palace [and placed] in the custody of Hegai, who was in charge of the women.

—ESTHER 2:8, AMP

Now the young woman pleased Hegai and found favor with him. So he quickly provided her with beauty preparations and her [portion of] food, and he gave her seven choice maids from the king's palace; then he transferred her and her maids to the best place in the harem.

—ESTHER 2:9, AMP

Now when the turn of Esther, the daughter of Abihail the uncle of Mordecai, who had taken her for his daughter, was come to go in unto the king, she required nothing but what Hegai the king's chamberlain, the keeper of the women, appointed. And Esther obtained favour in the sight of all them that looked upon her.

—ESTHER 2:15

And the king loved Esther above all the women, and she obtained grace and favor in his sight more than all the virgins; so that he set the royal crown upon her head, and made her queen instead of Vashti.

—ESTHER 2:17

And it was so, when the king saw Esther the queen standing in the court, that she obtained favor in his sight: and the king held out to Esther the golden sceptre that was in his hand. So Esther drew near, and touched the top of the sceptre.

—ESTHER 5:2

If I have found favor in the sight of the king, and if it please the king to grant my petition, and to perform my request, let the king and Haman come to the banquet

that I shall prepare for them, and I will do tomorrow as
the king hath said.

—ESTHER 5:8

Then Esther the queen answered and said, If I have
found favor in thy sight, O king, and if it please the king,
let my life be given me at my petition, and my people at
my request.

—ESTHER 7:3

And said, If it please the king, and if I have favor in his
sight, and the thing seem right before the king, and I be
pleasing in his eyes, let it be written to reverse the letters
devised by Haman the son of Hammedatha the Agagite,
which he wrote to destroy the Jews which are in all the
king's provinces.

—ESTHER 8:5

JOB

If you would [diligently] seek God and implore the compassion and favor of the Almighty.

—JOB 8:5, AMP

Thou hast granted me life and favor, and thy visitation
hath preserved my spirit.

—JOB 10:12

You would lie down with no one to frighten you, and
many would entreat and seek your favor.

—JOB 11:19, AMP

Will you show partiality for Him [and be unjust to me so that you may gain favor with Him]? Will you contend and plead for God?

—Job 13:8, AMP

His sons favor the poor [and pay his obligations], and his hands give back his [ill-gotten] wealth.

—Job 20:10, AMP

But the land is possessed by the man with power, and the favored and honorable man dwells in it.

—Job 22:8, AMP

You will also decide and decree a thing, and it will be established for you; and the light [of God's favor] will shine upon your ways.

—Job 22:28, AMP

He shall pray unto God, and he will be favorable unto him: and he shall see his face with joy: for he will render unto man his righteousness.

—Job 33:26

PSALMS

Blessed [fortunate, prosperous, and favored by God] is the man who does not walk in the counsel of the wicked [following their advice and example], nor stand in the path of sinners, nor sit [down to rest] in the seat of scoffers (ridiculers).

—Psalm 1:1, AMP

Kiss (pay respect to) the Son, so that He does not become angry, and you perish in the way, for His wrath may soon be kindled and set aflame. How blessed [fortunate, prosperous, and favored by God] are all those who take refuge in Him!

—PSALM 2:12, AMP

For thou, LORD, wilt bless the righteous; with favor wilt thou compass him as with a shield.

—PSALM 5:12

Where would I be if I did not believe I would experience the Lord's favor in the land of the living?

—PSALM 27:13, NET

For his anger endureth but a moment; in his favor is life: weeping may endure for a night, but joy cometh in the morning.

—PSALM 30:5

LORD, by thy favor thou hast made my mountain to stand strong: thou didst hide thy face, and I was troubled.

—PSALM 30:7

Hear, O LORD, be gracious and show favor to me; O LORD, be my helper.

—PSALM 30:10, AMP

Blessed be the LORD, for He has shown His marvelous favor and lovingkindness to me [when I was assailed] in a besieged city.

—PSALM 31:21, AMP

Blessed [fortunate, prosperous, favored by God] is he whose transgression is forgiven, and whose sin is covered.

—PSALM 32:1, AMP

Blessed [fortunate, prosperous, and favored by God] is the nation whose God is the LORD, the people whom He has chosen as His own inheritance.

—PSALM 33:12, AMP

O taste and see that the LORD [our God] is good; how blessed [fortunate, prosperous, and favored by God] is the man who takes refuge in Him.

—PSALM 34:8, AMP

Let them shout for joy, and be glad, that favor my righteous cause: yea, let them say continually, let the LORD be magnified, which hath pleasure in the prosperity of his servant.

—PSALM 35:27

Blessed [fortunate, prosperous, and favored by God] is the man who makes the LORD his trust, and does not regard the proud nor those who lapse into lies.

—PSALM 40:4, AMP

By this I know that thou favorest me, because mine enemy doth not triumph over me.

—PSALM 41:11

For they got not the land in possession by their own sword, neither did their own arm save them: but thy right hand, and thine arm, and the light of thy countenance, because thou hadst a favor unto them.

—PSALM 44:3

And the daughter of Tyre shall be there with a gift; even the rich among the people shall intreat thy favor.

—PSALM 45:12

By Your favor do good to Zion; May You rebuild the walls of Jerusalem.

—PSALM 51:18, AMP

God be gracious and kind-hearted to us and bless us, and make His face shine [with favor] on us—Selah.

—PSALM 67:1, AMP

But as for me, my prayer is to You, O LORD, at an acceptable and opportune time; O God, in the greatness of Your favor and in the abundance of Your lovingkindness, answer me with truth [that is, the faithfulness of Your salvation].

—PSALM 69:13, AMP

Will the LORD cast off for ever? and will he be favourable no more?

—PSALM 77:7

Restore us, O God; cause Your face to shine on us [with favor and approval], and we will be saved.

—Psalm 80:3, AMP

Restore us, O God of hosts; and cause Your face to shine on us [with favor and approval], and we will be saved.

—Psalm 80:7, AMP

Turn again [in favor to us], O God of hosts; look down from heaven and see, and take care of this vine.

—Psalm 80:14, AMP

Restore us, O Lord God of hosts; cause Your face to shine on us [in favor and approval], and we shall be saved.

—Psalm 80:19, AMP

Blessed and greatly favored are those who dwell in Your house and Your presence; they will be singing Your praises all the day long. Selah.

—Psalm 84:4, AMP

Blessed and greatly favored is the man whose strength is in You, in whose heart are the highways to Zion.

—Psalm 84:5, AMP

For the Lord God is a sun and shield; the Lord bestows grace and favor and honor; no good thing will He withhold from those who walk uprightly.

—Psalm 84:11, AMP

O LORD of hosts, how blessed and greatly favored is the man who trusts in You [believing in You, relying on You, and committing himself to You with confident hope and expectation].

—PSALM 84:12, AMP

LORD, thou hast been favorable unto thy land: thou hast brought back the captivity of Jacob.

—PSALM 85:1

Blessed and happy are the people who know the joyful sound [of the trumpet's blast]! They walk, O LORD, in the light and favor of Your countenance!

—PSALM 89:15, AMP

For thou art the glory of their strength: and in thy favour our horn shall be exalted.

—PSALM 89:17

And let the [gracious] favor of the LORD our God be on us; confirm for us the work of our hands—yes, confirm the work of our hands.

—PSALM 90:17, AMP

Light is sown [like seed] for the righteous and illuminates their path, and [irrepressible] joy [is spread] for the upright in heart [who delight in His favor and protection].

—PSALM 97:11, AMP

Thou shalt arise, and have mercy upon Zion: for the time to favor her, yea, the set time, is come.

—PSALM 102:13

For thy servants take pleasure in her stones, and favor the dust thereof.

—PSALM 102:14

Remember me, O LORD, with the favor that thou bearest unto thy people: O visit me with thy salvation.

—PSALM 106:4

Let there be none to extend mercy unto him: neither let there be any to favor his fatherless children.

—PSALM 109:12

Praise the LORD! (Hallelujah!) Blessed [fortunate, prosperous, and favored by God] is the man who fears the LORD [with awe-inspired reverence and worships Him with obedience], who delights greatly in His commandments.

—PSALM 112:1, AMP

A good man sheweth favor, and lendeth: he will guide his affairs with discretion.

—PSALM 112:5

How blessed and favored by God are those whose way is blameless [those with personal integrity, the upright, the guileless], who walk in the law [and who are guided by the precepts and revealed will] of the LORD.

—PSALM 119:1, AMP

Blessed and favored by God are those who keep His testimonies, and who [consistently] seek Him and long for Him with all their heart.

—PSALM 119:2, AMP

I intreated thy favor with my whole heart: be merciful unto me according to thy word.

—PSALM 119:58

Turn to me and be gracious to me and show me favor, as is Your way to those who love Your name.

—PSALM 119:132, AMP

Behold, as the eyes of servants look to the hand of their master, and as the eyes of a maid to the hand of her mistress, so our eyes look to the LORD our God, until He is gracious and favorable toward us.

—PSALM 123:2, AMP

Be gracious to us, O LORD, be gracious and favorable toward us, for we are greatly filled with contempt.

—PSALM 123:3, AMP

Blessed [happy and sheltered by God's favor] is everyone who fears the LORD [and worships Him with obedience], who walks in His ways and lives according to His commandments.

—PSALM 128:1, AMP

Behold, for so shall the man be blessed and divinely favored who fears the LORD [and worships Him with obedience].

—PSALM 128:4, AMP

Look to the right [the point of attack] and see; for there is no one who has regard for me [to act in my favor]. Escape has failed me and I have nowhere to run; no one cares about my life.

—PSALM 142:4, AMP

How blessed and favored are the people in such circumstance; how blessed [fortunate, prosperous, and favored] are the people whose God is the LORD!

—PSALM 144:15, AMP

How blessed and graciously favored is he whose help is the God of Jacob (Israel), whose hope is in the LORD his God.

—PSALM 146:5, AMP

The LORD favors those who fear and worship Him [with awe-inspired reverence and obedience], those who wait for His mercy and lovingkindness.

—PSALM 147:11, AMP

PROVERBS

So shalt thou find favor and good understanding in the sight of God and man.

—PROVERBS 3:4

For whoso findeth me findeth life, and shall obtain favor of the LORD.

—PROVERBS 8:35

He that diligently seeketh good procureth favor: but he that seeketh mischief, it shall come unto him.

—PROVERBS 11:27

A good man obtaineth favor of the LORD: but a man of wicked devices will he condemn.

—PROVERBS 12:2

Good understanding giveth favor: but the way of transgressors is hard.

—PROVERBS 13:15

Fools make a mock at sin: but among the righteous there is favor.

—PROVERBS 14:9

The king's favor is toward a wise servant: but his wrath is against him that causeth shame.

—PROVERBS 14:35

In the light of the king's countenance is life; and his favor is as a cloud of the latter rain.

—PROVERBS 16:15

Whoso findeth a wife findeth a good thing, and obtaineth favor of the LORD.

—PROVERBS 18:22

Many will intreat the favor of the prince: and every man is a friend to him that giveth gifts.

—PROVERBS 19:6

The king's wrath is as the roaring of a lion; but his favor is as dew upon the grass.

—PROVERBS 19:12

The soul of the wicked desireth evil: his neighbour findeth no favor in his eyes.

—PROVERBS 21:10

A good name is rather to be chosen than great riches, and loving favor rather than silver and gold.

—PROVERBS 22:1

He that rebuketh a man afterwards shall find more favor than he that flattereth with the tongue.

—PROVERBS 28:23

Many seek the ruler's favor; but every man's judgment cometh from the LORD.

—PROVERBS 29:26

Favor is deceitful, and beauty is vain: but a woman that feareth the LORD, she shall be praised.

—PROVERBS 31:30

ECCLESIASTES

I returned, and saw under the sun, that the race is not to the swift, nor the battle to the strong, neither yet bread to the wise, nor yet riches to men of understanding, nor yet favor to men of skill; but time and chance happeneth to them all.

—ECCLESIASTES 9:11

The words of a wise man's mouth are gracious *and* win him favor, but the lips of a fool consume him.

—ECCLESIASTES 10:12, AMP

SONG OF SOLOMON

To me, my love, you are like My [favorite] mare among the chariots of Pharaoh.

—SONG OF SOLOMON 1:9, AMP

I am a wall, and my breasts like towers: then was I in his eyes as one that found favor.

—SONG OF SOLOMON 8:10

ISAIAH

Let favor be shewed to the wicked, yet will he not learn righteousness: in the land of uprightness will he deal unjustly, and will not behold the majesty of the LORD.

—ISAIAH 26:10

When the boughs thereof are withered, they shall be broken off: the women come, and set them on fire: for it is a people of no understanding: therefore he that made them will not have mercy on them, and he that formed them will shew them no favor.

—ISAIAH 27:11

This is what the LORD says, "In a favorable time I have answered You, and in a day of salvation I have helped You; and I will keep watch over You and give You for a covenant of the people, to restore the land [from its present state of ruin] and to apportion and give as inheritances the deserted hereditary lands."

—ISAIAH 49:8, AMP

And the sons of strangers shall build up thy walls, and their kings shall minister unto thee: for in my wrath I smote thee, but in my favor have I had mercy on thee.

—ISAIAH 60:10

The LORD has anointed and commissioned me...to proclaim the favorable year of the LORD, and the day of vengeance and retribution of our God, to comfort all who mourn.

—ISAIAH 61:1–2, AMP

For we all have become like one who is [ceremonially] unclean [like a leper], and all our deeds of righteousness are like filthy rags; we all wither and decay like a leaf, and our wickedness [our sin, our injustice, our wrongdoing], like the wind, takes us away [carrying us far from God's favor, toward destruction].

—ISAIAH 64:6, AMP

JEREMIAH

"Only understand fully and acknowledge your wickedness and guilt, that you have rebelled (transgressed) against the LORD your God and have scattered your favors among strangers under every green tree, and you have not obeyed My voice," says the LORD.

—JEREMIAH 3:13, AMP

Then the LORD said to me, "Even though Moses and Samuel were to stand before Me [interceding for them], My heart would still not be [turned with favor] toward this people [Judah]. Send them away from My presence and out of My sight and let them go!"

—JEREMIAH 15:1

Therefore will I cast you out of this land into a land that ye know not, neither ye nor your fathers; and there shall ye serve other gods day and night; where I will not shew you favor.

—JEREMIAH 16:13

Please inquire of the LORD for us, because Nebuchadnezzar king of Babylon is making war against us. Perhaps the LORD will deal [favorably] with us according to all His wonderful works and force him to withdraw from us.

—JEREMIAH 21:2

Did Hezekiah king of Judah and all Judah put Micah to death? Did he not [reverently] fear the LORD and entreat the favor of the LORD? And did not the LORD relent and reverse His decision concerning the misfortune which

He had pronounced against them? But [here] we are [thinking of] committing a great evil against ourselves.

—JEREMIAH 26:19, AMP

"They will be carried to Babylon and they will be there until the day that I visit them [with My favor]," says the LORD. "Then I will bring them back and restore them to this place."

—JEREMIAH 27:22

Now it came about in the thirty-seventh year of the exile of Jehoiachin [also called Coniah and Jeconiah] king of Judah, in the twelfth month, on the twenty-fifth of the month, Evil-merodach king of Babylon, in the first year of his reign, showed favor to Jehoiachin king of Judah and brought him out of prison.

—JEREMIAH 52:31, AMP

LAMENTATIONS

The anger of the LORD hath divided them; he will no more regard them: they respected not the persons of the priests, they favored not the elders.

—LAMENTATIONS 4:16

EZEKIEL

Also bear your disgrace [as punishment], having made judgment favorable for your sisters, for [you virtually absolved them] because of your sins in which you behaved more repulsively than they; they are more in

97

the right than you. Yes, be ashamed and bear your disgrace, for you made your [pagan] sisters seem righteous.

—EZEKIEL 16:52, AMP

Arabia and all the princes of Kedar, they were your customers for lambs, rams, and goats [favored by you]; for these they were your customers.

—EZEKIEL 27:21, AMP

I will make them and the places around My hill (Jerusalem, Zion) a blessing. And I will make showers come down in their season; there will be [abundant] showers of blessing (divine favor).

—EZEKIEL 34:26, AMP

For, behold, I am for you, and I will turn to you [in favor], and you shall be cultivated and sown.

—EZEKIEL 36:9, AMP

And the nations will know [without any doubt] that the house of Israel went into exile for their great sin, because they acted treacherously against Me; and I hid My face (favor, blessing) from them. So I gave them into the hand of their enemies, and they all fell [into captivity or were killed] by [the power of] the sword.

—EZEKIEL 39:23, AMP

DANIEL

Children in whom was no blemish, but well favored, and skilful in all wisdom, and cunning in knowledge, and understanding science, and such as had ability in them to stand in the king's palace, and whom they might teach the learning and the tongue of the Chaldeans.

—Daniel 1:4

Now God had brought Daniel into favor and tender love with the prince of the eunuchs.

—Daniel 1:9

Until the Ancient of Days came and judgment was passed in favor of the saints of the Most High [God], and the time arrived when the saints (believers) took possession of the kingdom.

—Daniel 7:22, amp

Just as it is written in the Law of Moses, all this tragedy has come on us. Yet we have not wholeheartedly begged for forgiveness and sought the favor of the Lord our God by turning from our wickedness and paying attention to and placing value in Your truth.

—Daniel 9:13, amp

For ships of Cyprus [in Roman hands] will come against him; therefore he will be discouraged and turn back [to Israel] and carry out his rage against the holy covenant and take action; so he will return and show favoritism toward those [Jews] who abandon (break) the holy covenant [with God].

—Daniel 11:30, amp

HOSEA

Then I will give her her vineyards from there, and make the Valley of Achor a door of hope and expectation [anticipating the time when I will restore My favor on her]. And she will sing there and respond as in the days of her youth as in the day when she came up from the land of Egypt.

—HOSEA 2:15, AMP

Ephraim mixes himself with the [Gentile] nations [seeking favor with one country, then another]; Ephraim is a cake not turned [worthless; ready to be thrown away].

—HOSEA 7:8, AMP

He wrestled with the angel and prevailed; he wept [in repentance] and sought His favor. He met Him at Bethel and there God spoke with [him and through him with] us.

—HOSEA 12:4, AMP

NAHUM

All because of the many acts of prostitution of [Nineveh] the prostitute, the charming and well-favored one, the mistress of sorceries, who betrays nations by her acts of prostitution (idolatry) and families by her sorceries.

—NAHUM 3:4, AMP

HABAKKUK

Your eyes are too pure to approve evil, and You cannot look favorably on wickedness. Why then do You look favorably on those who act treacherously? Why are you silent when the wicked (Chaldean oppressors) destroy those more righteous than they?

—HABAKKUK 1:13, AMP

ZECHARIAH

And I looked up, and saw a man with a measuring line in his hand.

—ZECHARIAH 2:1, AMP

Now the people of Bethel had sent Sharezer and Regemmelech and their men to seek the favor of the LORD.

—ZECHARIAH 7:2, AMP

The inhabitants of one [city] will go to another, saying, "Let us go at once to ask the favor of the LORD and to seek the LORD of hosts. I will go also."

—ZECHARIAH 8:21, AMP

So many peoples and powerful nations will come to seek the Lord of hosts in Jerusalem and to ask the LORD for His favor.

—ZECHARIAH 8:22, AMP

So I [Zechariah] pastured the flock doomed for slaughter, truly [as the name implies] the most miserable of sheep. And I took two [shepherd's] staffs, the

101

one I called Favor (Grace) and the other I called Union (Bonds); so I pastured the flock.

—ZECHARIAH 11:7, AMP

I took my staff, Favor, and broke it in pieces, breaking the covenant which I had made with all the peoples.

—ZECHARIAH 11:10, AMP

I will pour out on the house of David and on the people of Jerusalem, the Spirit of grace (unmerited favor) and supplication. And they will look at Me whom they have pierced; and they will mourn for Him as one mourns for an only son, and they will weep bitterly over Him as one who weeps bitterly over a firstborn.

—ZECHARIAH 12:10, AMP

MALACHI

"But now will you not entreat God's favor, that He may be gracious to us? With such an offering from your hand [as an imperfect animal for sacrifice], will He show favor to any of you?" says the LORD of hosts.

—MALACHI 1:9, AMP

This is another thing you do: you cover the altar of the LORD with tears, with [your own] weeping and sighing, because the LORD no longer regards your offering or accepts it with favor from your hand.

—MALACHI 2:13, AMP

Chapter 7

FAVOR IN THE NEW TESTAMENT

MATTHEW

Blessed [spiritually calm with life-joy in God's favor] are the makers and maintainers of peace, for they will [express His character and] be called the sons of God.

—MATTHEW 5:9, AMP

If [the family living in] the house is worthy [welcoming you and your message], give it your [blessing of] peace [that is, a blessing of well-being and prosperity, the favor of God]. But if it is not worthy, take back your blessing of peace.

—MATTHEW 10:13, AMP

Blessed [joyful, favored by God] is he who does not take offense at Me [accepting Me as the Messiah and trusting confidently in My message of salvation].

—MATTHEW 11:6, AMP

Blessed [spiritually aware, and favored by God] are your eyes, because they see; and your ears, because they hear.

—MATTHEW 13:16, AMP

Then Jesus answered him, "Blessed [happy, spiritually secure, favored by God] are you, Simon son of Jonah, because flesh and blood (mortal man) did not reveal this to you, but My Father who is in heaven."

—MATTHEW 16:17, AMP

Then [Salome] the mother of Zebedee's children [James and John] came up to Jesus with her sons and, kneeling down [in respect], asked a favor of Him.

—MATTHEW 20:20, AMP

They sent their disciples to Him, along with the Herodians, saying, "Teacher, we know that You are sincere and that You teach the way of God truthfully, without concerning Yourself about [what] anyone [thinks or says of Your teachings]; for You are impartial and do not seek anyone's favor [and You treat all people alike, regardless of status]."

—MATTHEW 22:16, AMP

Then the King will say to those on His right, "Come, you blessed of My Father [you favored of God, appointed to eternal salvation], inherit the kingdom prepared for you from the foundation of the world."

—MATTHEW 25:34, AMP

LUKE

This is how the Lord has dealt with me in the days when He looked with favor on me, to take away my disgrace among men.

—LUKE 1:25, AMP

And the angel came in unto her, and said, Hail, thou that art highly favored, the Lord is with thee: blessed art thou among women.

—LUKE 1:28

And the angel said unto her, Fear not, Mary: for thou hast found favor with God.

—LUKE 1:30

Blessed [spiritually fortunate and favored by God] is she who believed and confidently trusted that there would be a fulfillment of the things that were spoken to her [by the angel sent] from the Lord.

—LUKE 1:45, AMP

For He has looked [with loving care] on the humble state of His maidservant; For behold, from now on all generations will count me blessed and happy and favored by God!

—LUKE 1:48, AMP

Glory to God in the highest heaven, and on earth peace to those on whom his favor rests.

—LUKE 2:14, NIV

And the Child continued to grow and become strong [in spirit], filled with wisdom; and the grace (favor, spiritual blessing) of God was upon Him.

—LUKE 2:40, AMP

And Jesus increased in wisdom and stature, and in favor with God and man.

—LUKE 2:52

He has anointed me . . . to proclaim the favorable year of the Lord [the day when salvation and the favor of God abound greatly].

—LUKE 4:18-19, AMP

He has anointed me...to proclaim the year of the Lord's favor.

—LUKE 4:18-19, NIV

Blessed [joyful, spiritually favored] is he who does not take offense at Me."

—LUKE 7:23, AMP

Whatever house you enter, first say, "Peace [that is, a blessing of well-being and prosperity, the favor of God] to this house."

—LUKE 10:5, AMP

Then turning to His disciples, Jesus said privately, "Blessed [joyful, spiritually enlightened, and favored by God] are the eyes which see what you see.

—LUKE 10:23, AMP

Now while Jesus was saying these things, one of the women in the crowd raised her voice and said to Him, "Blessed (happy, favored by God) is the womb that gave birth to You and the breasts at which You nursed!"

—LUKE 11:27, AMP

But He said, "On the contrary, blessed (happy, favored by God) are those who hear the word of God and continually observe it."

—Luke 11:28, amp

John

For the Law was given through Moses, but grace [the unearned, undeserved favor of God] and truth came through Jesus Christ.

—John 1:17, amp

If you know these things, you are blessed [happy and favored by God] if you put them into practice [and faithfully do them].

—John 13:17, amp

Jesus said to him, "Because you have seen Me, do you now believe? Blessed [happy, spiritually secure, and favored by God] are they who did not see [Me] and yet believed [in Me]."

—John 20:29, amp

Acts

Praising God, and having favor with all the people. And the Lord added to the church daily such as should be saved.

—Acts 2:47

And with great ability *and* power the apostles were *continuously* testifying to the resurrection of the Lord Jesus, and great grace [God's remarkable lovingkindness and favor and goodwill] rested richly upon them all.

—Acts 4:33, amp

Now Stephen, full of grace (divine blessing, favor) and power, was doing great wonders and signs (attesting miracles) among the people.

—Acts 6:8, amp

And delivered him out of all his afflictions, and gave him favor and wisdom in the sight of Pharaoh king of Egypt; and he made him governor over Egypt and all his house.

—Acts 7:10

Who found favor before God, and desired to find a tabernacle for the God of Jacob.

—Acts 7:46

But Paul chose Silas [who was again in Antioch] and set out [on his second journey], commended by the brothers to the grace and favor of the Lord.

—Acts 15:40, amp

And now I commend you to God [placing you in His protective, loving care] and [I commend you] to the word of His grace [the counsel and promises of His unmerited favor]. His grace is able to build you up and to give you the [rightful] inheritance among all those who are sanctified [that is, among those who are set apart for God's purpose—all believers].

—Acts 20:32, amp

Then a great uproar occurred, and some of the scribes of the Pharisees' party stood up and began to argue heatedly [in Paul's favor], saying, "We find nothing wrong with this man; suppose a spirit or an angel has [really] spoken to him?"

—ACTS 23:9, AMP

But after two years had passed, Felix was succeeded [in office] by Porcius Festus; and wishing to do the Jews a favor, Felix left Paul imprisoned.

—ACTS 24:27, AMP

And desired favor against him, that he would send for him to Jerusalem, laying wait in the way to kill him.

—ACTS 25:3

But Festus, wishing to do the Jews a favor, answered Paul, "Are you willing to go up to Jerusalem and stand trial there in my presence [before the Jewish Sanhedrin] on these charges?"

—ACTS 25:9, AMP

ROMANS

For God shows no partiality [no arbitrary favoritism; with Him one person is not more important than another].

—ROMANS 2:11

What then shall we say that Abraham, our forefather humanly speaking, has found? [Has he obtained a favored standing?]

—ROMANS 4:1, AMP

Now to a laborer, his wages are not credited as a favor or a gift, but as an obligation [something owed to him].

—ROMANS 4:4, AMP

Blessed and happy and favored are those whose lawless acts have been forgiven, and whose sins have been covered up and completely buried.

—ROMANS 4:7, AMP

Blessed and happy and favored is the man whose sin the Lord will not take into account nor charge against him.

—ROMANS 4:8, AMP

Therefore, [inheriting] the promise depends entirely on faith [that is, confident trust in the unseen God], in order that *it may be given* as an act of grace [His unmerited favor and mercy], so that the promise will be [legally] guaranteed to all the descendants [of Abraham]—not only for those [Jewish believers] who keep the Law, but also for those [Gentile believers] who share the faith of Abraham, who is the [spiritual] father of us all.

—ROMANS 4:16, AMP

But the Law came to increase *and* expand [the awareness of] the trespass [by defining and unmasking sin]. But where sin increased, [God's remarkable, gracious gift of] grace [His unmerited favor] has surpassed it *and* increased all the more.

—ROMANS 5:20, AMP

For sin will no longer be a master over you, since you are not under Law [as slaves], but under [unmerited] grace [as recipients of God's favor and mercy].

—ROMANS 6:14, AMP

But if it is by grace [God's unmerited favor], it is no longer on the basis of works, otherwise grace is no longer grace [it would not be a gift but a reward for works].

—ROMANS 11:6, AMP

What then? Israel failed to obtain what it was seeking [that is, God's favor by obedience to the Law], but the elect [those chosen few] obtained it, while the rest of them became hardened and callously indifferent.

—ROMANS 11:7, AMP

Who are you to judge the servant of another? Before his own master he stands [approved] or falls [out of favor]. And he [who serves the Master—the Lord] will stand, for the Lord is able to make him stand.

—ROMANS 14:4, AMP

1 CORINTHIANS

Now I have applied these things [that is, the analogies about factions] to myself and Apollos for your benefit, believers, so that you may learn from us not to go beyond what is written [in Scripture], so that none of you will become arrogant and boast in favor of one [minister or teacher] against the other.

—1 Corinthians 4:6, amp

But by the [remarkable] grace of God I am what I am, and His grace toward me was not without effect. In fact, I worked harder than all of the apostles, though it was not I, but the grace of God [His unmerited favor and blessing which was] with me.

—1 Corinthians 15:10, amp

The grace of our Lord Jesus [His unmerited favor, His spiritual blessing, His profound mercy] be with you.

—1 Corinthians 16:23, amp

2 Corinthians

…that is, that God was in Christ reconciling the world to Himself, not counting people's sins against them [but canceling them]. And He has committed to us the message of reconciliation [that is, restoration to favor with God].

—2 Corinthians 5:19, amp

"So come out from among unbelievers and be separate," says the Lord, "And do not touch what is unclean; and I will graciously receive you and welcome you [with favor]."

—2 Corinthians 6:17, amp

For you are recognizing [more clearly] the grace of our Lord Jesus Christ [His astonishing kindness, His generosity, His gracious favor], that though He was rich, yet for your sake He became poor, so that by His poverty you might become rich (abundantly blessed).

—2 Corinthians 8:9, amp

And God is able to make all grace [every favor and earthly blessing] come in abundance to you, so that you may always [under all circumstances, regardless of the need] have complete sufficiency in everything [being completely self-sufficient in Him], and have an abundance for every good work and act of charity.

—2 Corinthians 9:8, amp

They also long for you while they pray on your behalf, because of the surpassing measure of God's grace [His undeserved favor, mercy, and blessing which is revealed] in you.

—2 Corinthians 9:14, amp

Galatians

Am I now trying to win the favor and approval of men, or of God? Or am I seeking to please someone? If I were still trying to be popular with men, I would not be a bond-servant of Christ.

—Galatians 1:10, amp

I do not ignore or nullify the [gracious gift of the] grace of God [His amazing, unmerited favor], for if righteousness comes through [observing] the Law, then Christ died needlessly. [His suffering and death would have had no purpose whatsoever.]

—GALATIANS 2:21, AMP

So then those who are people of faith [whether Jew or Gentile] are blessed and favored by God [and declared free of the guilt of sin and its penalty, and placed in right standing with Him] along with Abraham, the believer.

—GALATIANS 3:9, AMP

You have been severed from Christ, if you seek to be justified [that is, declared free of the guilt of sin and its penalty, and placed in right standing with God] through the Law; you have fallen from grace [for you have lost your grasp on God's unmerited favor and blessing].

—GALATIANS 5:4, AMP

EPHESIANS

to the praise of His glorious grace and favor, which He so freely bestowed on us in the Beloved [His Son, Jesus Christ].

—EPHESIANS 1:6, AMP

Even when we were [spiritually] dead and separated from Him because of our sins, He made us [spiritually] alive together with Christ (for by His grace—His undeserved favor and mercy—you have been saved from God's judgment).

—EPHESIANS 2:5, AMP

For it is by grace [God's remarkable compassion and favor drawing you to Christ] that you have been saved [actually delivered from judgment and given eternal life] through faith. And this [salvation] is not of yourselves [not through your own effort], but it is the [undeserved, gracious] gift of God.

—EPHESIANS 2:8, AMP

Yet grace [God's undeserved favor] was given to each one of us [not indiscriminately, but in different ways] in proportion to the measure of Christ's [rich and abundant] gift.

—EPHESIANS 4:7, AMP

Fathers, do not provoke your children to anger [do not exasperate them to the point of resentment with demands that are trivial or unreasonable or humiliating or abusive; nor by showing favoritism or indifference to any of them], but bring them up [tenderly, with lovingkindness] in the discipline and instruction of the Lord.

—EPHESIANS 6:4, AMP

COLOSSIANS

Fathers, do not provoke or irritate or exasperate your children [with demands that are trivial or unreasonable or humiliating or abusive; nor by favoritism or indifference; treat them tenderly with lovingkindness], so they will not lose heart *and* become discouraged *or* unmotivated [with their spirits broken].

—COLOSSIANS 3:21, AMP

I, Paul, write this greeting with my own hand. Remember my chains. May grace (God's unmerited favor and blessing) be with you.

—COLOSSIANS 4:18, AMP

1 TIMOTHY

The grace of our Lord [His amazing, unmerited favor and blessing] flowed out in superabundance [for me, together] with the faith and love which are [realized] in Christ Jesus.

—1 TIMOTHY 1:14, AMP

I solemnly charge you in the presence of God and of Christ Jesus and of His chosen angels that you guard and keep these rules without bias, doing nothing out of favoritism.

—1 TIMOTHY 5:21, AMP

2 TIMOTHY

For He delivered us *and* saved us and called us with a holy calling [a calling that leads to a consecrated life—a life set apart—a life of purpose], not because of our works [or because of any personal merit—we could do nothing to earn this], but because of His own purpose and grace [His amazing, undeserved favor] which was granted to us in Christ Jesus before the world began [eternal ages ago].

—2 Timothy 1:9, amp

Preach the word [as an official messenger]; be ready when the time is right and even when it is not [keep your sense of urgency, whether the opportunity seems favorable or unfavorable, whether convenient or inconvenient, whether welcome or unwelcome]; correct [those who err in doctrine or behavior], warn [those who sin], exhort *and* encourage [those who are growing toward spiritual maturity], with inexhaustible patience and [faithful] teaching.

—2 Timothy 4:2, amp

Hebrews

Therefore let us [with privilege] approach the throne of grace [that is, the throne of God's gracious favor] with confidence and without fear, so that we may receive mercy [for our failures] and find [His amazing] grace to help in time of need [an appropriate blessing, coming just at the right moment].

— Hebrews 4:16, amp

Not like the covenant that I made with their fathers on the day when I took them by the hand to lead them out of the land of Egypt; for they did not abide in My

covenant, and so I withdrew My favor and disregarded
them, says the Lord.

—HEBREWS 8:9, AMP

How much greater punishment do you think he will
deserve who has rejected and trampled under foot the
Son of God, and has considered unclean and common
the blood of the covenant that sanctified him, and has
insulted the Spirit of grace [who imparts the unmerited
favor and blessing of God]?

—HEBREWS 10:29, AMP

By faith Moses, after his birth, was hidden for three
months by his parents, because they saw he was a beautiful and divinely favored child; and they were not afraid
of the king's (Pharaoh's) decree.

—HEBREWS 11:23, AMP

JAMES

Blessed [happy, spiritually prosperous, favored by God]
is the man who is steadfast under trial and perseveres
when tempted; for when he has passed the test and
been approved, he will receive the [victor's] crown of life
which the Lord has promised to those who love Him.

—JAMES 1:12, AMP

But he who looks carefully into the perfect law, the *law*
of liberty, and faithfully abides by it, not having become
a [careless] listener who forgets but an active doer [who

obeys], he will be blessed and favored by God in what he does [in his life of obedience].

—JAMES 1:25, AMP

My fellow believers, do not practice your faith in our glorious Lord Jesus Christ with an attitude of partiality [toward people—show no favoritism, no prejudice, no snobbery].

—JAMES 2:1, AMP

But if you show partiality [prejudice, favoritism], you are committing sin and are convicted by the Law as offenders.

—JAMES 2:9, AMP

You know we call those blessed [happy, spiritually prosperous, favored by God] who were steadfast and endured [difficult circumstances]. You have heard of the patient endurance of Job and you have seen the Lord's outcome [how He richly blessed Job]. The Lord is full of compassion and is merciful.

—JAMES 5:11, AMP

1 PETER

For this finds favor, if a person endures the sorrow of suffering unjustly because of an awareness of [the will of] God

—1 PETER 2:19, AMP

After all, what kind of credit is there if, when you do wrong and are punished for it, you endure it patiently? But if when you do what is right and patiently bear [undeserved] suffering, this finds favor with God.

—1 PETER 2:20, AMP

For the eyes of the Lord are [looking favorably] upon the righteous (the upright), And His ears are attentive to their prayer(eager to answer), but the face of the Lord is against those who practice evil.

—1 PETER 3:12, AMP

But even if you should suffer for the sake of righteousness [though it is not certain that you will], you are still blessed [happy, to be admired and favored by God]. Do not be afraid of their intimidating threats, nor be troubled or disturbed [by their opposition].

—1 PETER 3:14, AMP

Just as each one of you has received a special gift [a spiritual talent, an ability graciously given by God], employ it in serving one another as [is appropriate for] good stewards of God's multi-faceted grace [faithfully using the diverse, varied gifts and abilities granted to Christians by God's unmerited favor].

—1 PETER 4:10, AMP

After you have suffered for a little while, the God of all grace [who imparts His blessing and favor], who called you to His *own* eternal glory in Christ, will Himself complete, confirm, strengthen, and establish you [making you what you ought to be].

—1 PETER 5:10, AMP

By Silvanus, our faithful brother (as I consider him), I have written to you briefly, to counsel and testify that this is the true grace [the undeserved favor] of God. Stand firm in it!

—1 PETER 5:12, AMP

NOTES

INTRODUCTION
RIDICULOUS FAVOR

1. Google search, s.v. "favor," https://www.google.com/
search?q=favor&rlz=1C5CHFA_enUS690US690&oq=favor&a
qs=chrome..69i57j69i61j69i60j69i61j0l2.1033j0j4&sourceid
=chrome&ie=UTF-8.

2. "Favor of God," LearntheBible.org, http://www
.learnthebible.org/favor-of-god.html.

3. Merriam-Webster, s.v. "favor," https://www.merriam
-webster.com/dictionary/favor.

4. New Jerusalem Cathedral (@newjcofficial), "Get ready for
an avalanche of favor," Facebook, July 10, 2017, https://www
.facebook.com/newjcofficial/posts/1547012272039662.

5. Anita Alexander, "I Am Releasing Ridiculous Favor,"
z3news.com, March 8, 2017, https://z3news.com/w
/releasing-ridiculous-favor/.

6. Dea Warford, "Ridiculous Favor: Get Ready for a Fan-
tastic Miracle," EvangelistDeaWarford.org, http://www
.evangelistdeawarford.org/ridiculous-favor-get-ready-for-a
-fantastic-miracle.html.

7. Merriam-Webster.com, s.v. "ridiculous," https://www
.merriam-webster.com/dictionary/ridiculous.

8. Merriam-Webster.com, s.v. "ridiculous," https://www
.merriam-webster.com/thesaurus/ridiculous.

9. Jamie Rohrbaugh, "There Are Levels of Favor with God,"
FromHisPresence.com, December 3, 2015, http://www
.fromhispresence.com/there-are-levels-of-favor-with-god/.

CHAPTER 1
BUILDING FAITH FOR THE RIDICULOUS

1. David Cerullo, "God's Favor Is All You Need," Inspiration Ministries, https://inspiration.org/david-cerullo/strengthening-your-walk/gods-favor-is-all-you-need/.

2. E. A. Deckard, "The Favor of God Will Turn It in Your Favor," BlackPressUSA.com, http://www.blackpressusa.com/the-favor-of-god-will-turn-it-in-your-favor/.

3. Merriam-Webster.com, s.v. "astonish," https://www.merriam-webster.com/dictionary/astonish.

CHAPTER 2
THE KING'S FAVOR

1. Kevin Gerald, *Good Things* (Colorado Springs, CO: WaterBrook, 2015).

2. Michelle McClain-Walters, *The Esther Anointing* (Lake Mary, FL: Charisma House, 2014), 24.

3. Gloria Copeland, "The Favor of God Will Change Your Life," KennethCopelandMinistries.com, February 28, 2017, http://kennethcopelandministries.org/gods-favor-will-change-life/.

4. BlueLetterBible.org, s.v. "chayah," https://www.blueletterbible.org/lang/lexicon/lexicon.cfm?strongs=H2421&t=KJV.

Chapter 3
Four Ways to Favored Status

1. Goodreads.com, "Quotes About Favor," https://www .goodreads.com/quotes/tag/favor.

2. Merriam-Webster.com, s.v. "reconcile," https://www .merriam-webster.com/dictionary/reconcile.

3. Kong Hee, "The Key to Receiving God's Favor," Bible .com, https://www.bible.com/id/reading-plans/1968-kong-hee -gods-favor/day/1.

4. BrainyQuote.com, "Harold Warner Quotes," https:// www.brainyquote.com/quotes/quotes/h/haroldwarn194716 .html.

5. BrainyQuote.com, "James M. Barrie Quotes," https:// www.brainyquote.com/quotes/quotes/j/jamesmbar106441.html.

6. Joseph Prince, *Provision Promises* (Lake Mary, FL: Charisma House, 2013), as quoted in Joseph Prince, "Walking in God's Favor," Bible.com, https://www.bible.com/ reading-plans/1343-joseph-prince-walking-in-gods-favor.

Chapter 4
Simply Ask

1. Michelle McClain Walters, *The Anna Anointing* (Lake Mary, FL: Charisma House, 2017).

2. Judy Jacobs, "God's Favor Will Turn Everything Around," Inspiration Ministries, https://inspiration.org/christian-articles/ god-will-turn-everything-around/.

3. Henry D. M. Spence, *The Complete Pulpit Commentary*, vol. 6 (N.p.: Delmarva Publications Inc., 2014), Kindle.

CHAPTER 5
BENEDICTIONS, PRAYERS, AND
DECREES THAT RELEASE FAVOR

1. Joel Osteen, "Joel Osteen Explains the Mysteries of Unexpected Blessings in 'Break Out,'" Today.com, https://www.today.com/popculture/joel-osteen-explains-mysteries-unexpected-blessings-break-out-8C11306086.

2. Michelle J. Miller, "Winds of Favor," Facebook, July 24, 2017, https://www.facebook.com/michellejmiller01/posts/10212148584382898. Used by permission.

Made in the USA
Columbia, SC
01 November 2020